WOMAN AS CHURCH

The Challenge to Change

Claire C. Murphy SHCJ

Gill & Macmillan

Gill & Macmillan Ltd
Goldenbridge
Dublin 8
with associated companies throughout the world

0 7171 25505

Print origination by
O'K Graphic Design, Dublin

Printed in Malaysia

A catalogue record is available for this book from the British Library.

1 3 5 4 2

This book is dedicated to the members of Viatores Christi (Travellers for Christ), a lay missionary organisation based in Dublin. Over the past seventeen years as part of their preparation courses they have obliged me to study the history of the Church on mission, the development of the sacraments, the teachings of Vatican II, especially as they concern the role of the laity and attitudes towards members of other religions. As Viators returned from Asia, Africa, Latin America, North America and Eastern Europe they told of the needs of the poor in these areas and the efforts being made locally. All of this has provided a background from which to write this book.

ACKNOWLEDGMENTS

A special 'thank you' to my sister-in-law, Sheila Murphy, who cut weeks off the work by generously typing most of the script.

In a previous book (*An Introduction to Christian Feminism*) I outlined the various strands of feminism and showed where they agreed and differed. Since then I have continued to glean new insights from reading, attending seminars and sharing ideas with women and men interested in promoting Gospel values. I am especially indebted to Ben Kimmerling for her talks given at the Christian Feminist seminar on Sexuality held in Milltown, Dublin, on 29 May 1993 and to Soline Vatinel, co-founder of BASIC (Brothers and Sisters in Christ), for sharing with me the information she has gathered on the question of the ordination of women.

Gospel quotations throughout the book are taken from various translations. Jesus spoke Aramaic, the four Evangelists translated his teachings into Greek. Jerome translated from the Greek into Latin. Until the sixteenth century all translations of the Gospels into English were made from the Latin. So when we read the Gospels in English we are two or three translations away from what Jesus said and did. Each translation has its own emphasis depending on the words chosen. To avoid being dependent on any one translation I encourage the use of several and have quoted from translations best suited to the context in which they are used. The abbreviations are as follows: *The New Testament of our Lord and Saviour Jesus Christ* (Knox), *The Revised Standard Version* (RSV), *The Jerusalem Bible* (JB), *The Good News Bible* (GNB), *The New International Version* (NIV), *The New Revised Standard Version* (NRSV).

CONTENTS

1

The Turning Tide

The tide is turning. During the 1987 Synod of Bishops there were clear indications that the voices of Christian feminists were being heard:

> Women ask to be treated in a mutual relationship that is not condescending or paternalistic, that does not create passivity or dependency. Women wish to be treated in the way Jesus treated women: with trust and respect.
>
> *Archbishop Rembert Weakland of Milwaukee*

> The insufficient entry of women into the ecclesial environment is being experienced ever more as a fundamental failure of the Church. In no case are women only the *object* of pastoral ministry but rather *subjects*, responsible, in great measure and indispensably, in the life of the Church, and therefore as much in the spread of the faith as in the participation in pastoral ministry and *diaconia.* This awareness must be strengthened internally in the Church at every level and must be transformed into concrete action.
>
> *Bishop Gerhard Schwenzer of Oslo*

> Whether we like it or not feminism is now a challenge facing the Church. It can no longer be written-off as middle-class madness or an American aberration. Unfortunately, a considerable amount of alienation from the Church has already affected women in several countries. I'm not sure if we bishops realise how great is the anger of some who were once our friends. It will not be enough henceforth to issue grand statements unless we show progress in action.
>
> *Cardinal O Fiaich of Armagh*[1]

By 1994 Bishop Finnegan of Killala was saying: '. . . coming to terms [with feminism] is slowly beginning. . . . We are experiencing a slow and painful growth in attitudes and understanding on the part of the clergy, religious and lay people.'[2] That same year in his book *Crossing the Threshold of Hope* John Paul II wrote: '. . . the authentic theology of woman is being reborn . . . the particular genius of women is being rediscovered.'[3] In his *Letter to Women* issued in June 1995 before the UN Fourth World Conference on Women held in Beijing, Pope John Paul II acknowledged that historical conditioning had been an obstacle to the progress of women. Women, he continued, 'have often been relegated to the margins of society and even reduced to servitude. This has prevented women from truly being themselves and it has resulted in a spiritual impoverishment of humanity.' He went on to make his tide-turning apology: 'And if objective blame, especially in particular historical contexts, has belonged to not just a few members of the Church, for this I am truly sorry.' 'Yes,' he said, 'it is time to *examine the past with courage.*'

The Pope expressed his admiration for those women who fought for basic social, economic and political rights at a time when this was considered 'a lack of femininity . . . and even a sin!' And he declared that the journey is still unfinished, 'due to the many obstacles which, in various parts of the world, still prevent women from being acknowledged, respected and appreciated . . .' (n.6)

As a result of research into biblical interpretation and Church history undertaken by women scholars the minds of churchmen are slowly opening to a more inclusive understanding of Christ's mission. In the spirit indicated by John Paul II and in order to understand more fully why the Pope felt impelled to apologise to women, this book aims to give a brief overview of the Church's attitude to women over the past two thousand years and to indicate issues which as Church, in faithfulness to Christ's mission, we need to address today.

Feminism as a Christian Movement

It is a mistake to believe that the women's movement is solely about justice for women. It is more than that. It is about the future shape of the Church and society. Feminists see feminism as a spiritual movement concerned with meanings and values.

Feminists still consider patriarchy as the core problem for women and for society. By patriarchy is understood the cultural attitude which regards men as the norm for humanity. Women are seen as a secondary creation, created for the service of the male.

This attitude has been legitimised by the traditional interpretation of the Hebrew Scriptures. The opening chapter, Genesis 1, actually states that human beings, male and female, were created in God's own image and likeness. However, this passage was constantly ignored and the emphasis placed on Genesis 2 and 3 in which Eve is said to have been created as a helpmate for Adam, and after the Fall is told to be subject to her husband.

From the second to the fifth century the Fathers of the Church, influenced by these passages and by the prevailing patriarchal cultures, condemned women as the source of evil. Women were presented as temptresses and had to be kept in subjection for the protection of men. This preaching totally failed to appreciate the attitude of Jesus towards women. Thus throughout history we find that Gospel values and Church values are not necessarily the same.

Early in the twentieth century feminist scholars alerted Christian women to the fact that all was not well in their churches. Vatican II in the 1960s opened the way for Roman Catholic women to study Scripture and tradition to doctorate level. By the mid-1970s the findings of Christian feminist scholars began to circulate throughout the Church. Many clerical theologians came to appreciate the new perspectives and insights presented by these women. Others felt threatened, believing that the truth itself was being undermined. It is important to note that not all women in the Church are feminists, nor are all Christian feminists women. Young Catholic women do not feel the hurt and frustration of older women. The older women recognise that for years they gave allegiance to distorted patriarchal teachings and practices. In amazement the young ask, 'How come you were so unquestioning?' Western teenage girls are not usually feminists. They believe they have equal opportunities with men and are already involved with environmental and global issues. They will be in their thirties before they become aware of the 'glass ceiling' in the public domain, and before they experience the extent to which women are dependent in the domestic sphere.

For centuries men have defined what it is to be female and feminine. Feminists maintain that women are born female but are conditioned to be feminine on men's terms. Today they seek self-definition, self-affirmation, self-determination.

While their mothers still hope to see renewal brought about in the Church the young seek spiritual nourishment elsewhere. For them Vatican II is simply a dusty volume on a library shelf.

Women Examine the Past

Religion shapes inner attitudes. Inner attitudes affect public behaviour. This means that religious leaders exercise a tremendous influence on how people view themselves and others. Feminists see religion as dominated by male values and know that wherever there is domination injustices are bound to occur. Religions that consider women ritually unclean cause women not only to feel inferior but to be treated as such. In recent years many Catholic parents became aware of this when faced with the distress of small daughters who had been rejected as altar servers – these little girls were made to feel there was something shameful and unworthy about being female.

Women formed by religions that have a sacred book wonder if their Scriptures are used as tools of patriarchy. Christian feminists do not accept as divine revelation the traditional interpretations of Bible texts which are oppressive to women. They ask, 'Is the Bible based on divine revelation or on patriarchal proclamation?' They claim that the patriarchal tradition in the Church is not theological but is rooted in history and culture. Their women scholars have set themselves the task of reinterpreting the historical data in order to free the Gospel teachings from their cultural trappings. Jesus himself pointed out that not all scriptural teachings carry equal weight: 'You blind guides! Straining out gnats and swallowing camels!' (Mt. 23:24 JB).

Each text is interpreted within its historical context. For example, when they read '. . . women are to remain quiet at meetings. . . . If they have any questions to ask, they should ask their husbands at home' (1 Cor. 14:34–5 JB) the scholars ask if Paul was expressing the mind of Christ, or if he was asking the Greek converts to adhere to local custom so as to gain acceptance for the young Christian community.

It has been said that 'He who writes the history has the power.' In the Church, women for the most part have been omitted from the records. Therefore, the women scholars have had to seek other sources such as tomb inscriptions which name women as deacons and presbyters. They have had to probe into the sub-culture of the times and study the art, practices and devotions of their foremothers. They have begun to uncover the hidden history of women in the Church as they meet with women ministers, martyrs, scholars, mystics, writers, foundresses and social reformers.

Others ask: 'Do Church structures support or challenge sexism and classism?' Women know what it is like to be discounted and marginalised. Many have been hurt by their experience of Church. Christian feminists respond by seeking to bring about change through conversion. For women this means encouraging each other to claim not just equal rights with men, but more importantly, equal responsibilities.

The frustration felt by Christian feminists comes from their experience of themselves as disciples of Jesus and their growing awareness that something is out of sync. in the attitude of Church authorities towards women. A liturgy that renders women invisible and subsumes them under such terms as 'men', 'brothers', or 'sons' creates bewilderment. I was told of one little girl who on coming out of Mass asked, 'Mammy, why has God no daughters?' Church leaders who regard a wife as an obstacle to priestly ordination and who maintain that women cannot image Christ cause pain to many women at a deeply spiritual level. These women do not just belong to the Catholic Church, they *are* the Catholic Church, baptised into Christ and committed to carrying on his mission. They see feminism as a Spirit-inspired prophetic movement that is challenging the Church to become a more Christ-like community. They realise, of course, that their Church leaders and brothers had only a patriarchal language and society in which to fashion a Christian community. Yet they wonder how Christian men could have allowed a theology to develop that not only legitimised the subordination of women but distorted the Good News preached by Jesus.

Women doing Theology

Theology has been described as 'faith seeking understanding'. It is the work of the theologian, through the study of the tradition and reflection on the divine present in our lives, to continue an ongoing theologising that will enable us to understand more fully God's will for the world.

The Hebrew Scriptures came from within the Jewish culture. The Christian Scriptures were produced in the lands of the Mediterranean. The two most influential theologians of classical theology were the North African, Augustine Bishop of Hippo who wrote in the fifth century, and Thomas Aquinas, the Italian Dominican who taught in the thirteenth century and popularised the ideas of the pre-Christian Greek philosopher Aristotle. By the eighteenth century, with the rise of the Enlightenment, European theologians were forced to reconsider their teachings and, as they struggled to prove the existence of God, a modern theology was developed. All these theologies have one thing in common: they come from the male experience of life – as does Vatican II.

New theologies came to the fore in the twentieth century, as different groups of people reflected on God at work in their lives. The peasants of Latin America harboured no doubts about the existence of God. What they sought to understand was why a good and loving God allowed them to remain enslaved by poverty while their Christian masters lived in opulence. From their reflection on life in the light of the Gospel, liberation theology evolved. Meanwhile black theology emerged as theologians from the non-white races of the USA, Africa and Asia theologised on God in their relationships. Finally, as women reflected on their experience of the divine, feminist theology was born. These theologies attempt to heal the three great divisions in humanity: classism, racism and sexism. Paul declared that these divisions were redeemed in Christ. 'So there is no difference between Jews and Gentiles [racism], between slaves and free men [classism], between men and women [sexism], you are all one in union with Christ Jesus' (Gal. 3:28 GNB). In recent times Church leaders have acknowledged their mistake in condoning slavery and anti-Semitism. The time has now come to repudiate all sexist attitudes and practices within the Church.

Women undertaking theological studies have a difficult task ahead of them. Not only does the written tradition give very meagre data on women, but added to this is the fact that if their work is to be approved by the academic world they are obliged to follow the traditional approach and language which are the product of white male experience. Theology has imprisoned God in maleness. It is interesting to note that when the term 'mother' is used in reference to God no one goes away believing that God is female! However, feminist theology is not about changing nouns, but about presenting transcendence from another point of view. Christian feminists see how Jesus related to women and condemn the outrageous anti-woman statements made by the Fathers and later Church leaders. Women in study groups have thanked God for the insights of women scholars. One of them told me that feminism had helped mature her faith and had given her a new sense of responsibility for it – and this has been the experience of many women and men who have glimpsed the feminist vision.

Feminism and Men

Feminism is the outcome of women's reflection on their own experience as women. Obviously, therefore, men lack this essential ingredient at the level of experience. But once men grasp the insights of feminists and make them their own then they become pro-feminist. This is different from being in favour of equal rights for women, as this latter approach continues to accept patriarchal standards as the norm, and is about equal rights for women on men's terms.

Christianity is a religion of embodiment. The validity of human experience in theology is an accepted principle. Yet the Church has not given official recognition to the female experience of embodiment. Christian feminists point out that patriarchy presents motherhood as a lifetime vocation – she nurtures, whereas fatherhood is seen as an event – he begets. This attitude has helped to dehumanise men and to belittle fatherhood. Women complain that without any consultation with them, men make regulations that penetrate into women's wombs. Legal, medical and Church men speak as though they were the proprietors of women's bodies. Feminists say that men trained into these mind-sets have to learn to become brothers, not lords and masters.

The women's movement emerged when women became aware of the injustices condoned by patriarchy and it was driven by women's anger. Men have yet to go through the same process in order to free themselves from the limitations of patriarchy. There is no question here of diminishing men or apportioning blame. We are sisters and brothers brought up in the same culture and times. When discussing these matters one day an Irish bishop said to me, 'I feel as trapped as everyone else.' At a BASIC conference held in Dublin in March 1995 a priest bemoaned the fact that women were restricting their ministry to other women and pleaded: 'We need you to free us from our prejudices.' The women's responses varied. Some advised reaching out a supportive hand. Others suspected this was just a man who still wanted women to mother him!

Meanwhile, inspired by the changes brought about by the women's movement, men have started a separate movement that is rapidly gaining momentum. They believe that masculinity need not be patriarchal, but agree that there is an urgent need for men to learn new ways of exercising power. They seek to build fraternities based on renewed moral and spiritual values. For the most part the men's movement is seen as parallel to and supportive of the women's cause. However, some male groupings are accused of conducting an anti-feminist backlash, of endeavouring to promote the macho image and of trying to maintain the traditional gender roles.

Men are part of the problem. It is vital therefore that women seek to work as equals with men in bringing about change in both Church and society. Joan Chittister OSB when addressing women in the Dublin Mansion House in March 1995 pointed out that, 'Humanity walks on one leg, sees with one eye, thinks with half its brain – *and it shows.*'

Pause for Reflection

1. Identify how you feel about the changing attitudes towards women. Are you pleased, relieved, encouraged, apprehensive, irritated or indifferent, etc? Why?
2. What changes would a more Christ-like attitude towards women effect in the Church?

2

Attitudes Towards Sexuality

Male and female God created them (Gen. 1:27). Yet over the centuries femaleness became a huge source of misunderstanding for the male. Because of her biology, woman was regarded as 'a field to be sown', the property of the male, needing to be kept under his control. Gradually Church leaders gave legitimisation to this negative attitude towards women.

Jesus, the Word made Flesh

A reading of the Gospels shows that Jesus was at ease with the functions and limitations of his body. As village carpenter, and later as a travelling preacher he subjected himself to constant physical exertion. Yet he could admit to tiredness and thirst, as he did when he sat down at a well in Sychar and broke several taboos by asking a local woman for a drink (Jn 4:6–7). Again we read of him overcome with sleep, and that while at sea in a storm (Lk. 8:23).

Jesus spoke quite openly about private bodily functions. He insisted that no one was made unclean by what was eaten, as the food or drink went into the stomach and so passed out of the body; rather it was evil thoughts from within that caused impurity (Mk 7:18–23). Jesus is constantly recorded as eating and drinking socially, so much so that he tells us he was called 'a glutton and a drunkard' (Lk. 7:34). At other times he went out into the desert and endured long fasts (Mt. 4:2).

To touch was something Jesus did spontaneously. Again we find him breaking taboos as he took first Peter's mother-in-law and later Jairus' daughter by the hand. While healing a deaf man he put his fingers into the man's ears, spat and rubbed the spittle on his tongue (Mk 7:33). In the Temple, angered by abusive practices he made a whip from cords, drove out the cattle and sheep, threw over the tables of the money changers and scattered the coins all over the place (Jn 2:14–15). Nor did Jesus seem to mind being touched. He was jostled in crowds (Mk 5:31). Mary of Bethany felt free to handle and anoint his feet (Jn 12:1–8). When an unnamed woman anointed his head and his companions objected he defended her (Mk 14:3–9). At the Last Supper it is recorded that a disciple 'was sitting with his head against Jesus' breast; . . .' (Jn 13:25 Knox.)

In his relationships Jesus was as relaxed or confrontational with women as with men. During his visit to Martha and Mary he was obviously relaxed yet challenged Martha's attitude towards Mary (Lk. 10:38–42). Similarly when dining with Simon the Pharisee he challenged Simon's attitude towards 'sinners' (Lk. 7:36–50).

There is no record of Jesus' reactions to the physical changes he underwent at puberty..However, he is described at twelve years of age, the Jewish age for taking on adult responsibilities, as acting with great self-assurance and independence when unknown to his parents he remained on in Jerusalem discussing Scripture with the teachers of the law. The passage ends by telling us he returned to Nazareth where he continued to develop in mind and body (Lk. 2:40). Presumably he managed his sexual maturing with the same self-acceptance. The Gospels give no account of Jesus having a sexual involvement; what we do get is the picture of a person who has no emotional fear of the human body, his own or another's. Such is our Gospel heritage.

The Question of Clerical Celibacy

Despite this heritage, the Church seems never to have achieved a relaxed wholesome attitude towards our God-given sexuality. Around AD54, almost a quarter of a century after the death of Jesus, Paul wrote to the Corinthians in reply to a query. They wanted to know if it was worth their while getting married, as like Paul, they believed Jesus would return within their lifetime and that the world would end. Twice Paul declared that Jesus had given no teaching on the subject, but it was his own personal opinion that it would be wiser for single people to remain single and for the married to abstain from sexual intercourse. However, he added that if passion became too strong it was no sin to marry though it would be better to remain celibate (1 Cor. 7:25–40). This passage together with the remark made by Jesus that in heaven there was no giving in marriage (Mt. 22:30) led to the belief that celibacy was a holier way of life.

What led Paul to downgrade sexual activity within marriage? It has been suggested that in his anxiety to have Jesus accepted in the

West, Paul adapted Christian practice to the local cultures. Now in Greece the Stoic philosophy promoted detachment from pleasure. The Stoics called the Christians atheists, saying they were unable to maintain high standards of self-control. In response, some Christians started to live lives of strict self-denial. Meanwhile the Gnostics taught that spirit came from God and matter from the devil. They exalted celibacy and held marriage in low esteem. By the second century these views had infiltrated well into the Christian community. It is important to note that these negative attitudes towards sexuality came from Western philosophies and not from Jesus.

Judaism had not promoted celibacy, but by AD110 Ignatius of Antioch recorded the existence of Christians who chose to live as celibates. During this century women came to be regarded as the source of sin, e.g. Tertullian to women: 'Do you not know that you are Eve? . . . You are the devil's gateway . . .' Clement of Alexandria ordered women to go veiled so as not to lure men into sin. In AD306 the Synod of Elvira advised ministers to refrain from intercourse with their wives in preparation for serving at the Eucharist. So already by the fourth century even the lawful union with a woman within marriage caused a man to be ritually unclean.

By AD313 Christianity had so adapted to the Roman culture that it was no longer a threat to the State and was legalised by the Emperor Constantine, though he himself did not convert until many years later. The persecution of the Christians now ceased. Martyrdom had been considered the quick route to heaven by baptism of blood. Now celibacy came to be regarded as the more direct way to God and was looked upon as the new martyrdom. Large numbers of Christians, women and men, went into the deserts to live lives of self-denial. All sexual activity became associated with sin, and sex even within marriage was justified only as a means of procreation.

Married men continued to be ordained, but in AD325 at the Council of Nicaea it was decided that if a man was still single when he received the diaconate then he was no longer free to marry. This remains the ruling in the Orthodox Churches today.

By the start of the second millennium Rome's promotion of priestly celibacy added to the strain already in existence between the Eastern and Latin Churches. In 1054 the Orthodox Church finally separated from the Church of Rome. The First Lateran Council (1123) required celibacy of all priests. Reasons given for this decision vary: some believe it was because women were considered unclean, others say it had to do with property and the support of the priests' families. The priests of the Latin Church continued to resist the celibacy ruling, holding that it was against nature, and many priests and bishops continued to live in illicit marriages.

During the sixteenth century the Reformers attacked the celibacy law quoting 1 Tim. 4:1–5 in which those who forbid marriage are condemned as false teachers, for all that God has made is good. In response to the Reformation, the Council of Trent (1563) reaffirmed the celibacy rule. However, it was clear that laws alone would not ensure its acceptance. Therefore, seminaries were set up for the formal training of future priests and instruction was given on the spiritual aspects of consecrated celibacy.

With the coming of the Enlightenment in the eighteenth century marriage was seen as a basic human right. Thousands of French priests married, but by the next century when Napoleon signed the Concordat with Pope Pius VII in 1801 celibacy again became the norm for the French clergy. Finally, with the introduction of daily Mass, the rule which obliged priests to refrain from intercourse with their wives on the day before they celebrated the Eucharist made it impossible for them to fulfil their marriage vows. The Code of Canon Law of 1983 lays down that no man may be ordained unless he has first 'undertaken the obligation of celibacy' (Can. 1037). This promise of celibacy is made during the ceremony of ordination to the diaconate.

One priest writing anonymously in *The Tablet* of 9 July 1994 wrote: 'Too many priests who lack the gift of celibacy end up shouldering the discipline at the cost of serving the people.' Compulsory celibacy carries with it the occupational hazard of fearing intimacy and of never learning to love. Many people perceive their priests as emotionally stunted and sexually naïve. In the light of our growing understanding of patriarchal attitudes to women, psychological health, and human rights the celibacy rule is again being questioned.

For too long the influence of the Church Fathers with their fear of sex and distrust of women has permeated seminary training so that many priests have gone out into ministry with an unhealthy patronising or defensive attitude towards women. Priests not called to celibacy have learned to cope with their burden in various ways. Some simply anaesthetise the heart and become incapable of friendship. Others become workaholics, and others find compensation in things, e.g. drink, food, gadgets, hobbies, or in popularity, power, promotion. A minority seek comfort in sexual relationships.[1]

Their sufferings have led many Roman Catholics to question Church policy. They ask: Is it right to deny the Eucharist to vibrant Christian communities which have no celibate priest but do have trusted married catechists and Church leaders trained and financed to conduct prayer services and to interpret the Scriptures? They also ask: Why are priests, who have common-law wives and children, allowed to preside and consecrate at the Eucharist while men in lawful marriages are denied ordination? Scripture says that among the qualities required in a Church leader is faithfulness to one wife, good management of his children, a mature faith, the ability to preach and indifference to money and alcohol (1 Tim. 3:1–7). Clerical celibacy has never been compulsory in the Orthodox, Reformed or Anglican Churches.

Chastity, Celibacy, Virginity

At a seminar on 'Sexuality' organised by the Christian Feminist Movement, Ireland, in May 1993 the terms celibacy, chastity and virginity were discussed. It was pointed out that each one of us is unique and each of us leaves puberty as a complete person, not a half-person left looking for our 'other half'. It was also pointed out that the right to remain celibate is a basic right and that no one should be pressurised into marriage by family or peers.

Chastity, the practice of sexual restraint, enables one to control the sexual impulses. It was presented as a very freeing gift for both the married and the single, as it frees one to love without jealousy or the desire to sexually manipulate another. Chastity is an ideal for everyone no matter what their state in life.

With puberty, parental physical closeness ends. To deliberately choose a life of celibacy is to opt out of a second chance of having such physical closeness with the reassurance and comfort it can bring. Going without such intimacy requires careful psychological preparation if the personality is to survive undamaged.

But perhaps the greatest significance of the consecrated celibate for today should be her or his ability to model strong loving, affirming, non-genital relationships between the sexes. This would be a help not only to those who are single, but also to those who are married in their conduct of relationships outside of marriage. Unfortunately, most celibates have been trained to fear sexual attraction and to relate to others intellectually, thus cutting off the possibility of forming fully human friendships with all the emotions that involves.

Virginity usually carries the addition '*intacta*' when referring purely to physical virginity. Apparently in Greek and Roman society virginity implied social and psychological independence, a certain autonomy and integrity. It became a symbol for wholeness. The virgin is not driven by the desire to please, to win approval, or to control others. When discussing this point a woman said to me, 'I'm the mother of five children, yet in the past two years I've become aware of a deep virginity within myself. I regard it as the source of my integrity.' However, virginity can have a down-side. To be virginal might mean that one was closed to the penetration of another's love. A purely physical virginity has little value in itself; it could in fact indicate a fear of sex, or as one woman suggested 'A lack of opportunity'. Likewise, it was said, an undue anxiety to be married could signal an inability to come to terms with one's innate singleness, one's essential aloneness.

Women and Men are Different!

Apart from the external physical differences, newspaper and magazine articles are constantly claiming that research is now showing that the brains of women and men are also physically different. The *corpus callosum* is a cluster of fibres which connect the two brain hemispheres. Women have a far greater number of connecting fibres and so are quicker at processing information passing between the left and right sides of the brain. Babies are born with sexed brains. Anne Moir and David Jessel in their book *Brainsex,*[2] first published in 1989, report on some of the findings. Women's brains, they write, are better constructed for verbal and communication skills. They are more sensitive to touch and sound. Their eyes apparently have a wider arc of vision. The knowledge received is quickly processed by the brain which gives women the ability to interpret facial, tonal and emotional nuances. This may be the source of women's 'mysterious intuition'. It may also explain why witches were feared and misjudged. In 1484 Pope Innocent VIII issued a Bull permitting the torture of witches. These women were the local herbalists, healers and psychologists of their time. This facility to be aware of a situation from several perspectives can lessen decisiveness and earn for women the accusation that they are too easily distracted and lack concentration.

Men's brains, we are told, are more compartmentalised, with the areas controlling the emotions and reason well separated from each other. The activities of the left and right brain have fewer channels of communication and so men are less distracted by superfluous information – this enables them to be more concentrated. Men are better at processing spatial and abstract concepts, and at carrying out skills that require good eye-hand co-ordination. Other differences in brain formation have been identified but are not yet understood.

At puberty a new surge of hormones is released. Testosterone is the hormone that heightens the sexual impulse in both sexes. It also stimulates aggressive tendencies. It is not unusual for behaviour to change as a result of this new development and the young person, boy or girl, may become more aggressive or more withdrawn and moody. It is important for the young to realise they are not the slaves of their own sexual urges, and also that it takes time to learn the strength of their sexual passions which vary from person to person. They should be told that physical desire is involuntary and carries no guilt. To associate sin with these new bodily experiences is to spiritually cripple a person for life. To tell young people that their bodies can be an occasion of sin and that it is their duty to remove themselves from that occasion is to mock the Creator.

Rather as these latent sexual powers develop and the young person is entrusted by God with the power and responsibility of passing on life, public acknowledgment of her or his new adult status is called for. Many peoples around the world mark the transition from childhood with celebratory rituals after which the young person is treated as a responsible member of the community. Doctors keep reminding us that children do not produce babies. Adolescence is a modern Western concept. A society that prolongs adolescence beyond the early teen years has gone seriously askew. It treats young people as children and expects them to respond as adults.

It is commonly held that women and men have different sexual expectations in a relationship. Men who are less able to verbalise their feelings will try to express their love through sex and gifts, while women seek companionship and the sharing of thoughts as the central elements in a relationship. An ever-increasing number of men are becoming aware of a depth in relationships that they are missing out on. Around the world men are gathering in groups to learn how to get in touch with their feelings and to study the effects of patriarchy on them as well as on women. Many governments and organisations fund personal development courses for women. In Ireland unemployed men, who began to notice their wives and women friends becoming more self-fulfilled and involved in public issues, petitioned the government for grants to follow similar courses. There are now both private and government-sponsored seminars attended by men. When the men learn to listen and share, further seminars are planned for women and men to attend together.

Because men and women are different and have different strengths it is logical to encourage women and men to work together in partnership not only in the home, but in public life and in the Church. As we have seen, men find it easier to make quick decisions, while women having more data to process are slower but can usually come up with the more satisfactory solution. The example is given of the man who says: 'If you can't stand the heat get out of the kitchen.' So much for the person, he or she goes, but the environment remains unchanged for the successor. Now most women looking at the same situation would be more person-oriented and so would introduce change at the source of the problem. In this metaphor of the overheating kitchen, their solution would be to install a heat extractor. In other words, change the attitudes that accept as the norm oppressive traditions and destructive methods of conducting business. When men learn to respect and trust women's insights, the Church could become a far more wholesome and nourishing 'kitchen' to live and work in.

It is important to stress that these differences refer to the average. Obviously there are many women and men who do not conform to the average and who display the differences to a greater or lesser degree. It is also true that there are some roles which are better suited to one sex rather than to the other. The great injustice is that roles particularly suited to most women have been devalued by our patriarchal society. 'Women's work' is either low paid or not remunerated at all. This has given rise to the question: Do men consider the prostitute's work of greater social value than that of child rearing?

WOMANHOOD

Womanhood is what women experience it to be, not what men tell them it ought to be.

The women's movement is gaining respect world-wide and increasing numbers of people are accepting the justice of equal rights for women and girls. But there are also women and men who have yet to realise that the women's movement is about more than equal rights. A more accurate slogan would be: 'Equal rights for men and women and equal responsibilities for women and men.'

As a result of group reflection, research, study and analysis women are becoming more and more aware of just how broad and varied are their responsibilities in the Church and society. They are taking time to get in touch with their life experiences *as women.* It has been pointed out that women's minds were colonised by men so that women came to accept men's interpretation of their male experience as the whole truth about humanity. Our understanding of God, sin, grace, politics, business, education, international and interpersonal relationships, of achievement, success or failure all come from the male experience. The female mind perceives things differently. This was always known and was the subject of belittling jokes about women. Slowly the differences are beginning to be understood by both men and women and with this knowledge comes the vision of a fuller life for all people.

The Dewomanisation of Mary

Mary was a young Jewish woman who married Joseph, a carpenter, and soon after gave birth to her firstborn son. These are the recorded facts. Three of the Evangelists have no hesitation in indicating that Mary mothered a larger family. 'Isn't he the carpenter, the son of Mary, and the brother of James, Joseph, Judas, and Simon? Aren't his sisters living here?' (Mk 6:3 GNB). See also Mt. 13:55–56, Mt. 12:46–47, Mk 3:31–32, Lk. 8:19–20. These passages were written between AD64 and AD100, i.e. in the first century.

The second century saw the spread of Gnosticism which taught that as the body came from the devil, Jesus only had the appearance of being human. A mid-century document, the Book (or *Proto-Evangelium*) of James, said that Mary gave birth without breaking her hymen as the baby Jesus passed through her like a ray of light. In so writing the theologians sought to spare Mary the 'curse' of labour pains. Two hundred years later Augustine said of Mary that: 'as she conceived without sexual pleasure she gave birth without pain'. The fact that this belief was ever promulgated astonishes many women as they recall the sacredness of their own experience of bringing new life, out of pain, into the world. Unlike Jesus who focused on the joy of the event (Jn 16:21), the Fathers of the Church could not cope with the blood and labour involved, so they demeaned the process and presented Mary as a mere container. The writer of the Book of James was also unhappy with Mary in the role of wife and suggested that Joseph was a widower with a family, who took Mary under his protection. The 'brothers and sisters' of Jesus now became Mary's step-children. By the end of the fourth century Jerome decided that it was right and fitting for Mary's protector to be himself a virgin, and the 'brothers and sisters' became first cousins. Around the same time the monk Vinian taught that Mary gave birth in the normal way, and that virginity was not a higher state than marriage. He was excommunicated in AD391.

Cardinal Bellarmine SJ writing about Galileo in 1615 declared that to assert the earth revolves around the sun 'is as erroneous as to claim that Jesus was not born of a virgin'. However, on 28 August 1996 during a public audience, Pope John Paul II reaffirmed the virginity of Mary 'before, during and after' giving birth to Jesus and he repeated the traditional teaching that in Hebrew 'sisters and brothers' can have a broad meaning.[3]

The Female Body

Many women experience an inner terror when they hear of men, politicians, doctors or clergy, debating on or legislating for women's bodies. It can have the same effect on women as pornography. The female body is objectified, is regarded as subject to the control of men, while the woman herself, her feelings, her intellect are ignored. In 1847 James Young Simpson, professor of midwifery at the University of Edinburgh, was the first to give anaesthesia to women in labour. In 1853 English theologians condemned Queen Victoria's physician for anaesthetising her during childbirth quoting, 'In pain you shall bring forth children' (Gen. 3:16 RSV).[4]

Among some peoples, woman was believed to be the sole generator of life, and men regarded with awe her power to reproduce. The opposite view was held in the West, where it was held that the male alone possessed the 'seed of life'. To destroy semen was to kill. It was the nineteenth century before Von Baer discovered that the womb was more than an incubator and that the ovum provided half the genes necessary for human life. This new understanding of female biology enabled scientists to develop a pill that would help with problems of infertility in women. It also provided women with a means of controlling conception. While women welcomed the pill many found themselves under emotional pressure from men who expected them to be more sexually available. Today there is a growing awareness among women of the need to claim control over their own bodies.

In 1962 Pope John XXIII set up a commission to advise him and the Council Fathers on the moral implications of the various birth control methods then in use. 'By 1964 it had over sixty members, a third of them priests, the rest lay persons. It was to be increased later to include sixteen cardinals and bishops.'[5] When in 1951 Pope Pius XII allowed the safe-period as a means of birth control he abandoned the teaching that procreation was the sole purpose of the sexual act. Now the commission asked what moral difference there was between avoiding conception through the use of the safe-period or through the use of a condom. Four-fifths of the theologians agreed that there was no difference. Pope Paul then decided to withdraw the topic from the Vatican II agenda and to reserve the decision to himself. Despite the prohibition on further discussion in council, Cardinal Suenens of Belgium begged the bishops to avoid a new 'Galileo affair'.[6] In 1966 the commission members advised the Pope that the use of contraceptives was not contrary to the divine plan. However, a few members objected on the grounds that papal authority would be undermined by going contrary to previous papal teachings.[7]

Pope Paul followed the minority view and in 1968 published *Humanae Vitae* in which he condemned the use of any form of contraception. Many who continued as committed active members of the Church set aside this ruling and decided to follow their own consciences in the light of Vatican II: 'For they have in their hearts a law inscribed by God. Their dignity rests in observing this law, and by it they will be judged.'[8] This teaching is in turn based on Scripture, 'what the Law commands is written in their hearts. Their consciences also show that this is true, since their thoughts sometimes accuse them and sometimes defend them. This is the Good News I preach, on Judgement Day God through Jesus Christ will judge the secret thoughts of all' (Rom. 2:15–16 GNB).

Male intellectual answers are no longer sufficient. God has entrusted to women the responsibility for new life during the months of gestation. The emotional, physical, intellectual and moral experiences of women should form part of our common understanding of the faith. Meanwhile many a committed Christian woman makes lonely decisions in accordance with her own God-given conscience.

Sexual Orientation

Another area of sexuality now undergoing renewed investigation both within the Church and in medical circles concerns innate sexual orientation.

Heterosexuals, i.e. people sexually attracted to members of the opposite sex, are said to number about 90 per cent of the population. Up until recent discoveries in medical science this cross attraction was the only way of ensuring the continuance of the human race. The strength of this attraction varies greatly from person to person. The popular myth implied that all men had a high sexual drive while women had not. This belief left many individuals confused and worried. Some men confess to the strain experienced as they feign a need for sex, while highly sexed women say they become secretive and often vulnerable. Such women are labelled 'nymphomaniacs' and according to the Oxford dictionary have a 'morbid and uncontrollable sexual desire', while highly sexed men are called 'Casanovas' which the dictionary explains as a 'man engaging in promiscuous love affairs'. Note, the woman is described as a maniac, i.e. has a 'mental derangement' while the man is presented as a romantic.

Paedophiles are people whose sexual urges attract them to children. With the new focus on the rights of children, society is only now becoming aware of the lifelong hurt suffered by child victims. The distress of children both within families and within institutions has gone unrelieved for centuries. Yet child abuse is not always hidden – child prostitution and child pornography are advertised around the world. Research is showing how little is as yet understood about paedophilia. Present studies suggest that the condition cannot be cured but can be contained in a way similar to alcoholism.

Homosexuals and lesbians are men and women who are sexually attracted to members of their own sex. It is recognised that this may be a passing phase in young people as they learn to cope with their maturing sexuality. Or it can be a 'conditioned' attraction caused by a person's situation – for example, confined in a same-sex institution such as a boarding school, a prison or a harem. Change the situation and the individual will eventually find the opposite sex attractive. There is support and counselling available both within the Church and in society for anyone who needs help in making this transition.

Today there is a growing realisation that there is a third category known as the 'innate homosexual'. For them the same-sex attraction appears to be inborn, though like heterosexuals the strength of their sex drive varies from person to person. Such people, it is believed, are unable to become heterosexual and they are no longer regarded as suffering from a mental disorder. For them the counselling needed is to enable them to accept the reality of their nature. Though their sexual orientation may be natural it is not the norm, so they need support in dealing with the social prejudice they will meet.

While many people express bewilderment at the existence of homosexuality, the myths suggesting that those so oriented are sexually irresponsible and a danger to the young cause homosexuals and lesbians to live in fear of losing their livelihoods as nurses, teachers, social workers, etc. 'Destructive shame is the cause of suicide among many Christian homosexuals and lesbians. . . . They kill themselves not because they are gay but because they are not socially accepted and so cannot accept themselves.'[9]

All groups have sex criminals, but given their much larger numbers heterosexuals are a far greater threat to the vulnerable. It is up to heterosexuals to face their fear of the 'different', to free themselves of inherited prejudice, and to get rid of the stereotyped caricatures of the effeminate man and macho woman that are so often the butt of jokes. The homosexual community in the West has in recent years taken a more public profile in order to shatter myths, gain social justice, and support frightened young people who know that they are 'different'. Through its organisations it has engaged medical scientists and psychologists to enable these young people to understand the cause of their orientation and the prejudices it engenders.

One theory gaining credence is the result of studies done by the German scientist, Gunter Dörner and is described in the book *Brainsex.* This theory holds that 'innate homosexuality' is the result of brain formation. At conception a foetus is female having the XX chromosomes. By around six weeks, when the ovaries or testicles are due to form the male hormone testosterone is released, enters the brain tissue and in some foetuses changes the XX pattern to XY thus deciding the male sex of the future infant. Dörner suggests these changes take place in three stages. First, the section of the brain which decides the physical sex characteristics is affected. Next is the hypothalamus which controls sexual behaviour and differs in females and males. At this stage a lower concentration of androgens is likely to form a homosexual, while a higher level will form a lesbian. The third state affects a centre of the emotions causing greater aggression or timidity. This last stage is further affected at puberty. This three-stage theory could explain why homosexuals are more numerous than lesbians as the embryo starts off female and has to change to become male, and therefore there are more opportunities for the male norm not to be achieved.

There is reason to believe that outside interference in early pregnancy can also alter the sex formation of the brain. Studies show that women given male hormones to control toxaemia developed during pregnancy produced 'tomboy' daughters who grew up to be more ambitious and domineering than is the female norm. On the other hand, diabetic mothers with a history of miscarriages who were given artificial female hormones gave birth to sons who were diffident and avoided boisterous games, and some later entered into homosexual relationships. Dörner believes that amniocentesis, the test done on the fluid of the foetus, could detect homosexuality and if found in time a pre-natal injection could prevent its development. Many homosexuals feel threatened by this idea as it reminds them of the homosexuals disposed of in the Nazi gas chambers of the 1940s. Though not the norm, it would seem that 'innate homosexuality' can no longer be considered unnatural, any more than say colour blindness.[10]

Committed Christian homosexuals under the guidance of theologians and priest psychologists are exploring anew the Bible and Church teachings. The Gospels contain no specific teaching on homosexuality. The Hebrew Scriptures do comment on the subject and have influenced Christian teachings. 'You shall not lie with a male as with a woman; it is an abomination' (Lev. 18:22 RSV).

The Bible is the product of a patriarchal society. A patriarchal culture regards man as the norm for all humanity and woman as secondary, created for the service of men. Women were considered the property of men. Exodus 20:17 (JB), from which we get the ninth and tenth commandments, states: 'You shall not covet your neighbour's house. You shall not covet your neighbour's wife, or his servant, man or woman, or his ox, or his donkey, or anything that is his.' In their studies, Christian homosexuals question the extraordinary 'double standard' practised under patriarchy. Two angels in the form of two young men visited Sodom and stayed in the house of Lot. That night some of the men of Sodom surrounded the house and called for the young men to be brought out. They wanted to have sex with them. Lot went out closing the door behind him and said: 'Friends, I beseech you, do not perform such wicked deeds. Look. I have two virgin daughters. Let me bring them out to you and you can do whatever you wish with them. But refrain from touching these men as they are guests in my house, and I must protect them' (Gen. 19:1–11). For Lot it would seem the mass-rape of women was preferable to breaking the laws of hospitality or to homosexual acts.

A somewhat similar incident is recorded in Judges 19. A young concubine fled from her priest master who fetched her back from her father's house. They stayed overnight in Gibeah. Again the house was surrounded by local men who called out: 'Bring out the man within, we want to have sex with him.' The host came and pleaded: 'Do not engage in such immoral deeds. The man is my guest. I will give you his concubine and my daughter who is a virgin. I'll bring them out now and you can fulfil your desires with them.' The men would not listen, so the priest pushed his concubine outside. She was raped and abused all night. At dawn she fell by the door. . . . That morning her master opened the door and said: 'Get up. Let's go. But there was no response. So he placed the corpse across the donkey and started home.' Later he sought revenge for the insult done to *him*.

Genesis 38 tells the story of Tamar, daughter-in-law to Judah. She had been married to his eldest son who died childless. According to the levirate law the next son should marry her and beget a child in his brother's name. Onan refused and during intercourse withdrew, pouring 'the seed of life' on the floor. For this 'God slew Onan'. By law Tamar should now be married to the last and youngest son; instead Judah sent her back to her own people where as neither virgin, wife nor mother she would have no status. Hearing that Judah was coming to her town to sell sheep and knowing his habits, Tamar veiled herself as a prostitute. Judah negotiated sex with her leaving his signet, his cord and his staff as pledge of future payment. Three months later Judah was informed of his daughter-in-law's pregnancy. He gave the order: 'Take her and burn her to death.' Tamar sent Judah the signet, the cord and the staff. He recognised them and understood the message. Then he acknowledged that he had failed in his obligations to Tamar and ordered that she be set free. Here we have recorded that death was the punishment for destroying the male seed, and also for the daughter who acted the prostitute, but the man who used her was beyond reproach. These stories received their final editing as late as the sixth century before Christ. Stories such as these, plus other passages, cause Christian homosexuals to ask how authoritative is the Bible's teaching on sexual morality?

Jesus never referred to homosexuality save to declare that the people of Sodom would be treated more mercifully on the day of judgment than those of his native Galilee (Mt. 11:23–24). Paul saw homosexuality as a punishment for sin saying: God has given them over to shameful acts (Rom. 1:26–27). He lists homosexuals among idolators, adulterers, thieves, slanderers, drunkards, and the greedy, as those who will not enter the Kingdom (1 Cor. 6:9–10). Fifty years later his disciples wrote that the law is made for lawbreakers, the irreligious, murderers, homosexuals, kidnappers and liars (1 Tim. 1:8–11).

Today's studies are suggesting that for heterosexuals to perform homosexual acts is a perversion. But for the 'innate homosexuals' allowed by God to be so formed in the womb, to behave as homosexuals is to behave according to their nature. Catholic teaching accepts the homosexual person, but regards homosexual acts as 'intrinsically evil'. Innate homosexuals, not gifted with the call to celibacy, find it difficult to accept this teaching and see it as making a tyrant of God. Bishop David Konstant of Leeds while addressing the annual conference of Quest, the Catholic organisation for homosexuals in Britain, said, 'The whole Church must listen to you and you must listen to the Church – otherwise there is no dialogue.'[11]

There is a danger of equating sexuality with genitalia and sexual morality with genital acts. We are not simply people with sex organs but sexed people, and as such were created and redeemed. Sexuality is about relationships – it is about relationships that can enhance and affirm another rather than inhibit and damage. Innate homosexuals in the Christian community are trying to come to terms with their sexuality so that through it and not in spite of it, they can learn to be grace-filled persons for others.

Hermaphrodites are so called from the Greek myth in which the son of Hermes and Aphrodite came to share one body with the nymph Salamis. At birth these babies are hard to identify sexually as they combine within themselves both male and female characteristics. Hermaphrodites have both the XX sex chromosomes of the female and the Y of the male. At puberty these young people are usually subjected to the surgeon's knife to make them appear either male or female, as our society has not yet learned to accept people as they are. Some children with indeterminate sex appear to be male, are classified by society as male, yet experience themselves as female and so behave contrary to male norms. The same applies to infants who appear female in body but not in behaviour. Some of these young people as adults apply to have a sex change operation.

It took centuries to discover and understand the true nature of female reproductive biology. Obviously there is a lot more to discover and understand about the variations evident in human sexuality.

Spirituality and Sex

Sexuality is understood as the impulse that attracts one person to another; it is about relationships not acts. It is the power that starts one on the path to love and so to God.

Patriarchal culture in the Church and in society gave men control over wealth, property and women. The growing acceptance of women as co-equal partners with men has contributed towards a change in the Church's teaching on the purpose of sex. Procreation is no longer given as its primary purpose; instead, a loving relationship for mutual support comes first. The rejection of patriarchy includes the search for a new morality, not an acceptance of immorality. Our obsession with the morality of genital acts has placed the emphasis on masturbation, pre-marital sex, prostitution, contraceptives, abortion and homosexuality. Other areas of sexual immorality are now coming into focus: violence against women both domestic and public, gender injustice in education, in the workplace, in the home, and in the Church. Also the abuse of children: harsh discipline, slave labour, sex exploitation, discrimination against the girl child, the impoverishment of women and children. The challenge for Christians today is to avoid the a-moral position while resisting a return to the old repressive fears. New biological and psychological discoveries call for the 'natural law' to be redefined. Previous Church attitudes were formed around limited and at times an inaccurate understanding of human sexuality. The old negative views burdened many with scruples and put an enormous strain on some marriages, often causing frigidity or impotence.

Sexuality is God-planned and 'it is good'. When like Jesus we are comfortable in our bodies then we are free to love through them. Surely this is what the Incarnation is all about: embodied love leading us into the mystery of divine love.

> *Do not despise your body. For the soul is as safe in the body as in God's Kingdom.* (Mechtild of Magdeburg)

PAUSE FOR REFLECTION

1. (a) What would you consider the three most important ideas expressed in this chapter?
   (b) Which would you disagree with? Why?
2. Are there any Church attitudes towards sexuality that you think need to be re-examined? Why?

3

CHRISTIAN MARRIAGE

It was within marriage that many women were most burdened and guilt ridden. The Christian marriage ceremony required the woman to promise to obey her husband and the giving of the coin presumed that she would be financially dependent on him. It is only in the latter half of the twentieth century that attitudes towards the woman's role in marriage are being reassessed.

ANCIENT BIBLICAL LAWS

The Bible was produced within a patriarchal culture in which women were believed to have been created for the service of men. In the then common understanding of reproductive biology it was held that men possessed the 'seed of life' which had to be implanted into women to be incubated. Women were valued for their incubating capacity and were compared to land which the farmer sowed. Land and women were the property of men.

Deuteronomy 22:13–30, 24:1–5, 25:5–10, give some idea of the patriarchal management of women. The family had to retain proof of the woman's virginity at marriage. A husband who decided he no longer wanted his wife wrote out a bill of divorce and returned her to her family. If a husband died childless his brother was by law obliged to take the widow as an extra wife and bring up children in the dead man's name. If the woman was raped the rapist was forced to marry her and refused the right to divorce. At no time was it obligatory to consult the woman. Today, some women on reading these passages for the first time wonder if a liberating, just and compassionate God could possibly have inspired such regulations. They decide, No: these are the laws of men who have been damaged by sin. As one woman in a Dublin study group commented: 'It would be a cruel God who could give a woman intelligence if she was only meant to be a womb.'

The First Millennium

Marriage was a civil institution and regarded as a family affair. The arrangements were made between the parents; a male elder presided at the ceremony, while the father handed the bride over to the husband. Greek and Roman wives were mothers and household managers, not companions to their husbands. The marriage was expected to establish a stable environment for the begetting and nurturing of children. Christians followed the local marriage customs but added a spiritual significance to the union by declaring that the couple were 'married in the Lord'.

Paul introduced into the marriage agreement an element of mutuality which was extraordinary for his time. He said that the wife had the same rights over the body of her husband as he had over hers. This became known as the obligation to render the 'marriage debt or duty'. Paul regarded the 'containment of lust' as one of the purposes of marriage (see 1 Cor. 7:1–5). Marriage was not a high priority among these early Christians, as the Risen Christ was expected to return and to herald a new era in which there would be no 'giving in marriage'. Justin the Martyr (died AD165), who conducted a Christian school in Rome, tried to reconcile the pleasure of the marriage act with the faith and concluded that one undertook marriage purely to generate and raise children.

When in AD313 the Emperor Constantine legalised the Christian religion, the persecutions stopped and so the opportunity for a quick entrance into heaven through martyrdom was gone. Soon celibacy came to be proclaimed as the new martyrdom and was described as 'the higher call'. Though unintended, this attitude led to marriage being downgraded within the Christian community. However, the story of the creation of Adam and Eve forced the Church Fathers to acknowledge that sexuality was God-planned and therefore good, but they argued that the Fall had corrupted its purpose. They reaffirmed the beliefs of Paul and Justin by teaching that the sex act was justified only within marriage, and then only when performed for the procreation of children or the containment of lust.

Jerome (died AD420) was the first to translate the Bible into Latin. In the Book of Tobit it is recorded that on his wedding night Tobias asked his wife to pray with him for grace and protection, adding that he was not taking his wife out of lust. Then they lay together. In his translation Jerome added an extra verse. The story describes Tobias asking Sara to rise up and pray, to which Jerome added, 'to-day and tomorrow, and the day after, let us pray God for mercy. These three nights are set apart for our union with God; when the third is over, we will be joined in one, thou and I. We come of holy lineage; not for us to mate blindly, like the heathen that have no knowledge of God' . . . but 'only in the dear hope of leaving a race behind me, a race in whose destiny, Lord, may thy name be blessed for ever!' (Tob. 8:4–9 Knox). All Catholic translations of the Bible retained these additions up until Vatican II (1962–66). Recently an elderly Australian woman told me that the priest who presided at her wedding made her promise to give her wedding night to God in prayer. Her husband-to-be was obliged to agree. Later when the babies arrived they had a wholly different experience of night vigils and realised that there were other ways of glorifying God.

By the fifth century the Eastern and Western Churches developed different customs regarding the wedding ceremony. The East placed it in a more religious context, the priest took over part of the father's role by crowning the bride and joining the hands of the couple. The priest came to be seen as the minister of matrimony. The Latin Church continued with a more secular approach.

Augustine (died AD430) commenting on the text, 'Behold I was born in iniquity and in sin did my mother conceive me' (Ps. 51:5 NCE) declared that sexual pleasure was the source of original sin. Despite this belief he also held that there were sacramental elements in a marriage between Christians. Pope Leo the Great (died AD461) stated that all conjugal intercourse was tainted by sin. This prevailing negative attitude towards sexuality made it hard to consider the possibility of divine grace being mediated through marriage.

The collapse of the Roman Empire in 476 resulted in the people looking to Church leaders, especially the pope, to take on responsibility for maintaining social order, and so political and military powers were entrusted to the papacy. Gradually marriage too came under the control of Church law rather than civil law. Pope Gregory the Great (died AD604) reversed Leo's view that married intercourse was tainted with sin by stating that marital sex is sinless when used for procreation. Attitudes to sex continued to see-saw within the Church throughout the first millennium.

The Teutonic peoples of Northern Europe followed a more legalised way of life. With their conversion to Christianity in the eighth century we read of marriage contracts between Christian families. The contract was considered essential to secure property.

It was the ninth century before we get our first description of a marriage solemnised in Church. It was written by Pope Nicholas I who in his writings stressed that this was not the common practice nor was it Church law. Christians did not consider the wedding ceremony part of the ritual of the Church, so marriages continued to be celebrated within the home.

The Second Millennium

According to the law of the Roman Empire a marriage came into being with the mutual consent of the couple. Among the Northern European tribes it was the sexual act which established the marriage. The Byzantine Emperor Justinian in the sixth century had defined marriage as 'a union of a man and a woman, and a communion of the whole of life'. The latter phrase was found to be ambiguous, did it mean 'till death do us part' or did it refer to an equal sharing in lifestyle? By the middle of the twelfth century the Church had reached a compromise and marriage became a two-stage process. First, the ceremony of mutual consent, second, the act of intercourse. Only when both stages were completed was the marriage deemed indissoluble. It was also in keeping with the Roman law that the Church laid down that the aims of marriage were the procreation and nurture of children, plus mutual support and the containment of lust. The theologian Hugh of Saint Victor (died 1142) advocated what he called a Josephite Marriage after Saint Joseph. It was considered a more spiritualised form of marriage in which the husband and wife lived as brother and sister.

Throughout the first millennium baptism and the Eucharist had been spoken of as sacraments. In the twelfth century the sacraments were reconsidered and Peter Lombard, Bishop of Paris (died 1160), decided to list marriage among the sacraments of the Church. As a sacrament marriage was now completely under the control of the Church authorities, who not only laid down regulations for the ceremony of mutual consent but also for the conduct of the marital act. Intercourse was forbidden on all Sundays and holy days, during Advent and Lent, and for three days before receiving Holy Communion; also during menstruation or pregnancy because 'you don't sow the same field twice', and finally for a period after childbirth. It was believed that children conceived during the forbidden times would be born physically or mentally damaged. Yet, a wife was admonished to submit to her husband even on Good Friday to prevent his going elsewhere, and provided she took no pleasure in the act she remained sinless.[1] In

1198 Pope Innocent III wrote to the Archbishop of Armagh in Ireland, advising him not to reprimand mothers who entered the Church after childbirth, but rather to praise those who out of respect stayed away for a period.

With sexual love so debased by the Church a young man could no longer associate sex with the woman he loved; she became 'the Lady', was mentally placed on a pedestal and idealised. Prostitutes were used for sex. Healthy wholesome womankind ceased to be acknowledged.

Pope Alexander III (died 1181) directed that a priest should be present at the ceremony of consent to ensure that the young couple were truly free and not pressurised by either family to enter into the marriage. He taught that the free act of consent made the marriage valid, while the act of intercourse made it indissoluble. Hence the formula: 'A marriage freely consented to and consummated cannot be annulled.' The Fourth Lateran Council (1215) in its concern to prevent forced marriages decreed that private marriages were to be no longer recognised. Though clandestine marriages continued, marriage in a church became the sign that the sacrament had been administered.

During the thirteenth century the Albigensians condemned marriage and denounced the body as evil. Responding to these views the Dominican theologian Thomas Aquinas (died 1274) declared that 'marriage in the Lord' was a true sacrament as 'power in marriage is given to the husband to use his wife for procreation, so too that grace is given him without which he could not do this appropriately'.[2] Duns Scotus (died 1308) taught that the grace of the sacrament was administered by the couple to each other.

By the sixteenth century the Church needed reform on several fronts and a split became evident in the understanding of Christian marriage. During the Reformation years the reformers returned to the earlier understanding of marriage as a civil arrangement 'according to the order of nature', but continued to recognise that the couple were 'married in the Lord'. While acknowledging that the couple were setting up a Christian household they held that the Church should not interfere in civil matters. The main body of Western Christianity, i.e. the Roman Catholic Church, again proclaimed marriage to be a sacrament at the Council of Trent (1545–63). It refused to recognise any marriage not witnessed by a priest and two members of the Church. It also declared that consecrated virginity and celibacy were the more blessed states.

The Pauline and Petrine Privileges

When Jesus said, 'What God has joined together, let no one separate' (Mt. 19:6) he was, of course, speaking of Jewish marriages. However, when writing to the Corinthians, Paul introduced a teaching of his own concerning Christian marriage. He stated categorically that it was not a teaching of the Lord. He said that if a spouse converted to the faith and the non-believer was willing to live peacefully with the convert then the marriage should continue as the baptised spouse might convert the unbaptised partner. But if the non-believer was not willing to live peacefully, then the new Christian was free to marry another Christian and the previous marriage was automatically dissolved for 'It is to peace that God has called you' (1 Cor. 7:12–15 NRSV). This Pauline privilege became part of Church law in 1199 and since the sixteenth century has been used extensively as the Church expanded east and south into other cultures. The Church 'in favour of the Faith' claims the power to dissolve the marriage of an unbaptised couple if one of the partners is converted to Catholicism. Pope Paul III in 1537 ruled that in the case of a polygamous convert the man was to retain his first wife. Some time later Pope Pius V in 1571 allowed the husband to choose any wife willing to be baptised.

This reminds me of an old chief in Ogoja, Nigeria. He had four wives, then elderly, and numerous children all of whom had been baptised and educated as Catholics. They were headmasters, teachers, nurses, etc., and themselves raising Christian families as active members of the Church. But the chief had refused to be baptised. Curious, I asked why, seeing that he had taken such trouble to bring his children up in the faith. 'Ah. How could I face God if I sent any of my wives away? They have reared their children well, been companions to each other, I could not disturb and degrade them now. No, I will meet God unbaptised but with my duty done and he will be pleased to see me.' He died four months later.

Just as Paul interpreted the teachings of Jesus to meet the needs of the converts in Corinth, so too the Church today interprets the Scriptures according to current insights and situations. Marriages not dissoluble under the Pauline privilege may be dissolved under the Petrine privilege. The power of this privilege rests on the words of Jesus to Peter at Caesarea Philippi: 'I will give you the keys of the kingdom of heaven, whatever you bind on earth shall be considered bound in heaven; whatever you loose on earth shall be considered loosed in heaven' (Mt. 16:19 JB). Again it is regarded as a privilege 'in favour of the Faith'. The Petrine privilege has been exercised in the dissolution of marriages between baptised and non-baptised persons. Both the Pauline and Petrine privileges are regarded as favours not rights, and the Church imposes many regulations before granting them.

Divorce, Separation and Annulment

Another means of dissolving a marriage is through divorce. In Deuteronomy 24:1 the husband is to give his wife a bill of separation if, because she no longer pleases him, he sends her away. This passage was often debated by the rabbis. At the time of Jesus the school of Shammai held that the wife could be sent away only for adultery, while the school of Hillel maintained that the passage allowed her to be dismissed for many other reasons, such as bad cooking or even ageing. When some Pharisees asked Jesus, 'Is it lawful for a man to divorce his wife for any cause?' (Mt. 19:3) in his fairly long reply Jesus stated that the only valid reason was for adultery. Matthew repeated this exemption (Mt. 5:32). Thus Matthew presents Jesus as a supporter of the Shammai teaching. In their references to divorce neither Luke 16:18 or Mark 10:11–12 record any exemption.

Throughout the centuries Christian scholars have tried to interpret the Matthean exemption. Some say that Matthew, in recording the teachings of Jesus some fifty years after his death, added the exemption so as to conform to Roman law which gave both the husband and the wife the right to initiate a divorce. Others hold that in making only the one condition Jesus was saying that women were entitled to greater security and a more stable marriage. Yet others point out that the word used for adultery is '*moicheia*', but that in the exemption phrase Matthew uses the word '*porneia*' which means unlawful sexual intercourse and so could refer to incest, bestiality, prostitution or concubinage. Basil the Great (died AD379) who spent most of his teaching life defending the faith against Arianism, allowed divorce on the Matthean exemption. The Orthodox and Reformed Churches follow the same ruling.

The Roman Catholic Church does not permit divorce, not even for unfaithfulness. In recent years some bishops have within their own dioceses adopted what is called the pastoral solution whereby the divorced person who has remarried in a civil ceremony may come to church to have the marriage blessed and thereafter receive the sacraments. These bishops argue that though lifelong faithfulness is the ideal, Jesus in dealing with human weakness in any form always offered a second chance. The Vatican has not approved of this practice.

When the Church allows a separation it frees the couple to 'sever the common conjugal life' (Can. 1152). It is granted to meet the needs of various situations; for example: if a spouse has committed adultery, is living a criminal life, is practising cruelty either physical or mental, is a danger through mental illness or has a contagious disease that could be passed to the other through intercourse, is causing spiritual harm or is squandering the family funds. The couple is expected to live together again if the reason for the separation has ceased.

The Catholic practice of granting annulments is a cause of great bewilderment and hurt for many Catholics. An annulment declares that the vows made by the couple were null and void and that therefore they had at no time lived within the married state. The focus is on the moment of consent and the investigators try to discover if either partner was not in fact making a true act of free consent with full understanding as to what that consent entailed. It may be that the bride had no knowledge of the act of intercourse, or that as the vows were being exchanged one partner intended to continue in an extramarital affair. It may be that the couple were too immature to undertake a lifelong commitment, etc. It also happens that after the vow ceremony a couple discovers that for physical or psychological reasons the marriage act cannot be performed and so the marriage is not capable of being consummated. When an annulment is granted many years after the ceremony of consent and after the birth of several children it raises anxious questions within the Catholic community.

Sex in Marriage

No passage in the Christian Scriptures equated marriage with procreation. However, the Church Fathers' interpretation of the Fall reduced sexuality to a necessary evil justified only for procreation within marriage, and led to the teaching Church concerning itself with regulating the exercise of the marital act. A text book published soon after Vatican II and intended as a guide for priests in administering the sacraments, gives the 'authorised norms' regarding the obligations, abuses, physical and moral aspects of performing the marital act. It is stated that, 'the right to the body of one's spouse is precisely what is transferred in marriage'.[3] 'Difficulties which can arise and which are intrinsic to marriage are not of themselves sufficient cause to deny the debt, such as the large number of children born, past experience of a difficult pregnancy or birth, fear of another miscarriage, etc.'[4] There follow a number of prohibitions which if practised should be confessed in the sacrament of penance. But the spirit of Vatican II got through in the text when the author wrote: 'Marital love is uniquely expressed and perfected through the marital act, which within marriage is noble, worthy and meritorious when under the influence of charity.'[5]

Among these many directives for the conduct of married sex is the presumption that celibate theologians have the greater authority with which to pronounce on Christian marriage than do the couples who administer its sacramental grace and who encounter the divine through their marriage. This clerical presumption perhaps explains the present backlash in the Church against celibate priests who are sexually active as heterosexuals, homosexuals or paedophiles. The initial reaction from Church leaders to recent scandals was to point out that doctors, teachers, parents and others were also found wanting. This, of course, is true but there is a huge difference; only the clergy presumed to regulate the intimate actions of the married couple.

There is a growing realisation in the Church that clerical leadership has failed married couples. As more married people study and do theology they are highlighting the fact that to reduce sexuality to a merely physical act is to make it no longer a human act and therefore not a moral act. Many couples say they experience intercourse as a means of fostering wholeness and healing far beyond the understanding of celibates, and see marriage as embodied, incarnate love.

In accepting the rhythm method of birth control the Church no longer holds that intercourse is for procreation alone. For many Roman Catholics contraception has ceased to be a moral question and is seen rather as a problem of Church authority. Those who use contraceptives believe they are not dissenting but acting responsibly. They explain that intellectual input does not provide sufficient data on which to make a moral decision, physical and emotional responses are also essential ingredients, and in the final analysis the Church teaches that conscience rules supreme and that individuals must make their own moral choices. Intercourse and pregnancy need no longer go together which means that young women today have choices and responsibilities unknown to their mothers or grandmothers. While theologians can afford to take decades to debate the new issues arising, these women have only their years of fertility and so risk taking decisions contrary to present Church teaching. They believe that the Spirit of truth inspires the whole Church and that official confirmation comes later.

Financial Dependency

The Industrial Revolution caused couples to leave the large extended family of the farms or villages and go to the towns. These 'nuclear families' of just father, mother and children isolated in small houses near factories or offices suited the new work patterns of men. Life changed drastically for the wife who no longer contributed to the family income. For her a proposal of marriage became akin to a job offer. The terms were unspoken but understood. 'I'll provide house and food, you clean and cook.' Parenting came to mean mothering as husband and wife worked in different spheres, he in the public sphere, she in the home. The long working hours meant they saw little of each other, so it was possible to distinguish between her marriage and his. Some enjoyed romance and love, for others it was fidelity, duty and routine intercourse. Marriage was presented as a woman's goal. Her identity, her name, her status were achieved through her husband. Many women found and still find their fulfilment in the lifestyle of what came to be called the 'housewife'. This occurs only where the woman has made a free choice and is not taken for granted in the roles of wife and mother. If such a marriage ends in desertion or a legal separation, the woman usually finds herself greatly impoverished not only emotionally but materially as well. The desertion or separation has revealed how economically dependent she was.

In the manual on marriage already mentioned, it is stated that the spouses are equal as persons and have equal rights to the body of the other. But the husband is head of the family, the wife is his helpmate, owes him reverence and obedience, and must follow him to wherever he fixes his abode. They have different roles, he is provider and protector, she is the nurturer of the children with the duty to maintain a comfortable home.[6] Many women now see this as a system based on the assumption that a woman's right to an adequate standard of living depends on her ability to please her husband. Two very competent young Dublin women have told me that they 'slept with the boss'. They meant that when extra money was needed, maybe for a scout uniform or an adult education class, it often entailed humouring the husband-provider. These women loved their husbands and enjoyed caring for their small children, but they were aware that child-rearing was a temporary phase and were already preparing for future careers and a more equal relationship with their husbands.

Until there is some economic equality between men and women, perhaps along the lines of a basic income for all, it is doubtful if there will ever be the level of economic independence that enables mutuality. As long as there is financial dependence there is emotional dependence. It is important not to confuse dependency with love. Thousands of wives do not know what their husbands earn. They are given housekeeping money and that is that. To survive with dignity the financially dependent wife can unconsciously become a skilled manipulator. This does irreparable harm to the woman's personality and to the woman/man relationship. The Church's teaching on the just distribution of wealth needs to be applied within the marriage commitment and to be stressed during the wedding ceremony. It is important also to recognise that for some men the role of sole provider becomes too great a burden and in desperation they desert.

A New Theology for Marriage

Couples today find that marriage as expounded by celibates is not how Christian marriage is lived. Personal experience is a valid source from which to do theology. A married priest, once spiritual director in a seminary but no longer in official ministry, shared with a group of us how on the Christmas Eve after the birth of their first child he and his wife had been kept up most of the night trying to pacify the crying baby. On Christmas morning the exhausted mother remained in bed while he took the still fractious infant downstairs to change, wash and feed her. All the while his irritation grew. This was not how he had planned his Christmas morning. For a week he had been looking forward to his annual quiet hour of meditation on the mystery of the Incarnation. At this point the parents present guffawed. Our priest friend confessed that it was a week later before he realised that he had failed to recognise the Christmas reality present in his kitchen. He regretted the years of priestly spiritual training that had been so abstract and theoretical.

A new, more positive theology of marriage is in the process of developing, based on the experiences of married couples, especially women. For some Catholic couples being disciples of

Christ is an important element in their marriage, but one for which they feel they get little support from Church leadership. They find marriage is still regarded as the lesser vocation. When studying at a theological institute a woman friend of mine was told by a seminarian, 'As a married woman you wouldn't understand about being filled with God.' Another remarked, 'We religious give ourselves 100 per cent to God.' She asked, 'Is the love I give my husband and children taken from God?' She wondered how these young priests-in-training could ever minister to married people and asked, 'Is ministry to be only one way?'

While not denying the charism of celibacy, the charism of marriage must become central in the Church. The Church is the people of God, yet spiritual leadership has become the preserve of celibates with the result that our spirituality for marriage is puritanical – denying the gift of pleasure. The Song of Songs is never read at Mass, nor are homilies preached in which God's presence in loving married intercourse is mentioned. The saints are given to us as models for Christian living yet so far no couple has been canonised. Mary and Joseph are offered as models but we are taught that they lived as brother and sister. Married individuals have been canonised, but not a couple. Yet most Christians are called to live their lives as partners in marriage and as such to fulfil Christ's command to 'love one another'.

The graces available in the sacrament of matrimony are not sufficiently used for the good of the couple, the family or the community. At a seminar on Christian Marriage organised by 'Sophia', Dublin, in February 1993 it was concluded: 'That the power of love in marriage is the greatest untapped source for redemption in the Church. In a unique way married couples can lead us to a fuller understanding of God's unconditional love and forgiveness.' A new theology of marriage is awaited and only married Christians can bring it to birth. At the end of the seminar the following recommendations were made: (1) that at each Sunday Mass an intercessory prayer be offered for the support of married couples; (2) that one Sunday of the year be designated Marriage Vocation Day. At Mass couples could renew their vows and a married couple would be asked to preach the homily; (3) that the parish invite married couples to participate in a Resource Ministry by sponsoring couples planning to marry, welcoming new couples into the parish, forming support groups for couples, for those in interfaith marriages and for those whose marriages have failed; (4) finally, to minister by giving talks on Christian marriage in seminaries, local schools and youth clubs.

The speed of cultural change in our day is new and it affects our life commitments. Marital breakdown is one of the greatest challenges facing the Church at present. Previous preparation for marriage prepared couples for their respective roles. Today the need is for training in how to sustain relationships. For the modern couple, if the relationship breaks down there seems little point in remaining together just to carry out roles. They are aware that children flourish only where the atmosphere between adults is loving, respectful and caring, and that this is the security children need. It has been noted that generally it is the wife who seeks the separation. Some believe this is because women are rejecting their wifely and maternal roles, others insist it is because women are no longer willing to be regarded as property.

In his Apostolic Letter on *The Dignity of Women* John Paul II wrote: 'in Christ the mutual opposition between man and woman – which is the inheritance of sin – is essentially overcome.'[7] Commenting on Ephesians 5:22, 'Wives be subject to your husbands as to the Lord', the Pope stressed that this subjection is to the Lord and mutually to each other. He adds that the Letter to the Ephesians describes the old order of sin which Christ has redeemed. In a footnote he lists seven other passages in the Letters that should be interpreted from this redemptive point of view. They are Col. 3:18, 1 Pt. 3:1–6, Tit. 2:4–5, Eph. 5:22–24, 1 Cor. 11:3–16 and 14:33–35, 1 Tim. 2:11–15.[8]

This change of attitude in the teaching Church is also evident when we compare the 1917 Code of Canon Law with that of 1983. The 1917 Code stated that the primary end of marriage was the procreation and nurture of children, and that the secondary end was mutual support and the remedying of concupiscence. In the 1983 Code the ends are reversed and what was a contract has now become a covenant of relationship which 'by its very nature is ordered to the well-being of the spouses and to the procreation and upbringing of children. . . .' (Can. 1055). Marriage had been seen as an arrangement to secure a stable environment for the nurturing of children. Husband and wife were undertaking specific roles to ensure that end. Now the Church teaches that the covenanted relationship between the couple is at the core of the marriage.

Inculturating Christian Marriage

Christian marriage developed within the Roman culture and was later influenced by Germanic customs. The universal imposition by the Church of this form of marriage is now questioned, and there is a growing desire for the inculturation of Christian marriage in Africa, Asia and Latin America.

I will always remember my first lesson in inculturation. It took place in eastern Nigeria in 1956. At that time there were not many secondary schools for girls, so when the opportunity for a place was offered, the girl arrived in First Year irrespective of her age. Quite a number were already promised in marriage. That first week after my arrival, the sacrament of matrimony was the subject for the religious education class. We followed the text book and all was quiet and orderly until we came to the quote from Genesis, 'Therefore a man leaves his father and mother and clings to his wife, and they become one flesh' (Gen. 2:24 NRSV). This was greeted with screams, drumming on the desks, riotous laughter and shouts of 'No, no, no!' I soon learned that for these young women the important relationships were vertical from grandmother to child to grandchild. The culture was that of the extended family and of polygamous unions.

In most African cultures marriage is a process. In the Catholic Church it is a two-stage process; first the vows of consent are exchanged, later the marriage is consummated. In parts of Africa the process is often reversed. After the initial arrangements between the couple and their families the elders bless and pray over the couple, then the act or acts of intercourse take place over a period of time. If the woman becomes pregnant the marriage is understood to be blessed by God and the ceremony of the exchange of vows is celebrated. If the woman does not become pregnant the couple seek medical help, they reconsider the marriage commitment and they are free to seek new partners. This reversal of the process from the Roman model has caused heartbreak for many a European missionary priest. One committed Catholic bridegroom explained to me that though he and his wife loved and chose each other, and both had university education, their marriage would have been put under intolerable family pressure to split if they failed to produce children. This reality leads some theologians to question the validity of the vow ceremony if it is conducted knowing that the couple may have the reservation that if no children are born of the marriage they will separate.

Perhaps the most impressive wedding I ever attended took place in a small Ibibio village. The couple belonged to one of the local evangelical churches. When we arrived at their chapel we discovered that there were no bridesmaids. Instead the couple were sponsored by three couples who had lived in Christian marriage for ten or more years. The minister questioned the bride and bridegroom on their understanding of Christian marriage and if they hesitated on any question a sponsor would supply the answer. It was an education for all present and made clear that marriage was not a private but a community affair. After the exchange of vows the couple were reminded of the joys and difficulties of the marriage commitment and advised to take any difficulties they might encounter to their more experienced sponsors. If at any future time they wished to separate they were first to discuss the reasons with each of the six sponsors and seek their unanimous agreement.

The Wedding Ceremony

In the West some of the present wedding customs come from an earlier culture and today seem meaningless. For example, the father of the bride 'gives her away'. Many hold that there is no place for such a 'transfer of property' gesture in any Christian marriage. Some women find the present Catholic ritual so patriarchal and clericalised that it just makes them angry. The recent Irish Episcopal guidelines for the ceremony directs that, 'After the giving of the ring comes the "giving of the gold and silver" when the husband places a coin in the bride's hand as a token of all he possesses.' Note 'ring' is in the singular and the giving of the coin suggests it is right and fitting for the bride to become financially dependent. Both the giving of the ring and the giving of the coin take place during the same solemn moment before the altar and before the official witnesses. Yet, as many a married woman knows, neither Church nor society took the coin promise seriously and even the family home remained the property of the husband.

The Church teaches that for a marriage to be valid the couple must at the exchange of vows accept: (a) that the commitment is for life; (b) that each intends to be sexually faithful to the other; (c) that neither will refuse to generate children. A rite is important in itself as it forms attitudes and values that might not otherwise be expressed. To emphasise the fact that the bride and bridegroom are the ministers of the sacrament it is important that the couple be seen to conduct the exchange of vows. More often nowadays, the priest-witness stands alongside the other official witnesses. This is the moment when it would be more appropriate for family elders to preside and later for a married couple to give the homily. Some liturgists suggest that the entire rite take place before, not within, the Eucharistic celebration as there it is the priest's role to preside. Ritual is not window dressing, it should shape our minds, hearts and behaviour. Once the sacrament of matrimony is recognised as the responsibility of the baptised, and that the Christian home is a sacred place where God's freeing love is administered for the enrichment of the whole community, then a new era of Christian renewal will have begun in the Church.

The Domestic Church

Vatican II described marriage as 'a community of love'. Jesus is recorded as saying that their love for one another is the sign by which his disciples would be known (Jn 13:35). For Christians, marriage is not only a shared life, it is also a shared discipleship. Some Christian couples have pointed out that Jesus sent his disciples out two by two, and so they regard their wedding ceremony as a commissioning service.

Once, when discussing the sacrament of matrimony with a group of married women, one older woman said: 'I feel so cheated. I'm so annoyed with myself for never questioning my deeper feelings, for often I felt there was a deep well of holiness underlying my marriage but I did not know how to tap into it.' Another woman shared how when she was preparing to go to a Holy Hour in her local church, leaving her husband to mind the children, she suddenly realised God's love was present in her living room and by enjoying an evening with her family God would be glorified.

By insisting on the vow ceremony taking place in a church building the Church leadership is affirming that marriage is not a private affair but is significant to the life of the community, for what is meant by Church takes place within the home which from ancient times was called the domestic Church. There, where two or three are gathered in Christ's name, Christ is present (Mt. 18:20). When marriage is accepted as a sacrament and the couple acknowledged as the ministers of sacramental grace then it follows that the 'priesthood of the baptised' is exercised within the home. Unfortunately, marriage seems to be what some call 'the forgotten sacrament'.

Pause for Reflection

1. What would you suggest are the three most important points to be agreed on when a couple prepare for Christian marriage?
2. Name three ways in which the sacramental role of the domestic Church could be enhanced.

4

The Development of the Christian Priesthood

A look at the development of an all-male celibate cultic priesthood that not only took over ministry but also jurisdiction should provide a useful background from which to consider ministry for women in the Church.

Priesthood in Judaism

In Israel, priesthood had nothing to do with personal call, ordination or pastoral care. It was a religious function inherited within the tribe of Levi to whom Moses had entrusted the care and protection of God's sanctuary (Num. 3:5–13).

When the Israelites finally settled in Israel the priests became important cultic figures serving in the Temple in Jerusalem and exercising considerable influence at the court of the king. Zadok is named as one of the priests at David's court who became chief priest under Solomon. His descendants were known as Sadducees, the priestly caste frequently mentioned in the Gospels. By the time of Jesus the high-priesthood had assumed a political status, for with the collapse of the monarchy the high priest had become the chief representative of the Jewish people answerable to Rome.

Another religious group frequently met with in the Gospels is that of the rabbis, that is the teachers of religion. They were not priests. Most belonged to the strict Jewish sect known as the Pharisees. While the Sadducees accommodated themselves to the Roman occupation and retained their wealth and influence as a priestly aristocracy centred around the Temple, the Pharisees opposed Roman rule and were found teaching in the synagogues throughout the land.

Jesus was not a Jewish priest. He was not of the tribe of Levi and did not qualify to carry out the Temple rituals. Instead he became a preacher and was popularly called rabbi and prophet. Jesus lived and died a faithful Jew. He started a religious renewal movement within Judaism and proclaimed what he termed the 'reign of God'. This was not associated with sacred places but with doing the will of God and thereby transforming both self and society (Jn 4:21–24). Those accepting the reign of God would be recognised not by titles or distinctive dress but by their compassionate love. There would be no more domination/submission relationships, the last would be first, the leaders would act as servants, the weak would realise that they were strong. Discipleship was open to everyone who repented of wrongdoing and underwent the inclusive ritual of baptism by water, not the male ritual of circumcision. His was to be a peace movement acting as a leaven in the world (Mt. 13:33). It was the Sadducees, the priestly caste, who recognised the threat Jesus offered to their way of life. Caiaphas, who was high priest that year, said: 'What fools you are! Can't you see it is better that one man die for the people than that our whole nation be destroyed?' (Jn 11:49–50).

Interpreting the Scriptures

The Greek word *hermeneutic* refers to the interpretation of Scripture. The hermeneutic of acceptance refers to traditionally held interpretations such as those which present Jesus as the founder of a new religion. These interpretations present Jesus as instituting seven sacraments and at the Last Supper ordaining twelve men whom he set up as a hierarchy to govern his Church. It teaches that the roles of bishop, priest and deacon date from the first community in Jerusalem and that the hierarchical structure was observed from the beginning throughout the whole Church.

In the twentieth century, when Christian women got the opportunity to study the Bible to scholarship level, some have pursued what they term a 'hermeneutic of suspicion'. This means that they question the centuries-old interpretations of male celibate priests in order to discover if they have been excessively coloured by a patriarchal culture. They suspect that the Bible might reveal new insights if studied from a feminist perspective. Male scholars have joined in the new research and now we have a third phrase, the 'hermeneutic of recognition'.

The Twelve

A reading of the first three Gospels shows that Jesus, after prayer, chose twelve men to be his close companions in mission. He empowered them with the gift of healing and sent them out to preach the Good News (Mk 3:13–19, Mt. 10:1–4, Lk. 6:12–16). Luke also reports Jesus as saying that the twelve will judge the twelve tribes of Israel (Lk. 22:30). Commentators vary as to how they interpret this passage but the reference to the twelve tribes is seen as Jesus maintaining a continuity with the Covenant. However, the question is raised as to who exactly were the twelve. Matthew (10:1–4) and Mark (3:16–19) name them as Simon Peter, his brother Andrew, James and John the sons of Zebedee, Philip, Bartholomew, Thomas, Matthew, James son of Alphaeus, Thaddaeus, Simon the Zealot, and Judas Iscariat. Luke (6:12–15) omits Thaddaeus and instead names Judas son of James.

John makes only one passing reference to the twelve. 'One of the twelve disciples, Thomas (called the Twin) was not with them when Jesus came' (Jn 20:24 GNB). John describes the call of Andrew, Peter, Philip and Nathanael (1:35–51). He names Judas Iscariot when Mary of Bethany is criticised for wasting expensive perfume on Jesus (Jn 12:4), and he tells us that Simon Peter, Thomas, Nathanael, the sons of Zebedee and two other disciples were out fishing when they saw the Risen Christ on the shore of the Sea of Tiberias (Jn 21:1–14). So in all John identifies eight male disciples of Jesus. He constantly refers to 'the disciple whom Jesus loved' but never actually names him or her.

Luke repeats his list, now down to eleven, when he describes them as present with Mary and other women awaiting the promised descent of the Holy Spirit. It was here in the upper room that Peter suggested replacing Judas, and Matthias was chosen (Acts 1:12–16). Yet after Pentecost the twelve disappear out of history and we learn no more of Bartholomew, Philip, Andrew, James the son of Alphaeus, Thaddaeus, Simon the Zealot, Judas the son of James, or Matthew.

Like John, Paul makes one passing reference to the twelve. '. . . he appeared first to Cephas and secondly to the Twelve' (1 Cor. 15:5 JB). Two questions are constantly asked by students: (1) Why do we not have a twelve today? (2) Why after Pentecost did the twelve cease to have any great relevance for the young Christian community? Seventy years after the death of Jesus, when John's Gospel was written, their names were not even recorded.

The Apostles

There is a problem about equating the twelve with apostleship. In 1 Cor. 15:6 Paul says that after appearing to Peter and the twelve, Jesus appeared to more than five hundred witnesses at once, some of whom were still alive while others have since died. Later, he appeared to James and then 'to all the apostles' (1 Cor. 15:7 JB). Here Paul seems to distinguish between Peter and the twelve apostles, and James and the other apostles, and he goes on to claim that he received his own apostleship directly from the Risen Christ. Paul also writes of those outstanding apostles Andronicus and Junia, 'my compatriots and fellow prisoners who became Christians before me . . .' (Rom. 16:7). Throughout his Gospel John never refers to apostles, only to disciples.

The Last Supper

The priesthood is said to have been conferred upon the twelve at the Last Supper. In Mark's account Jesus arrived with the twelve. But at table when asked who was to betray him he answered, 'It is one of the Twelve' (Mk 14:20 JB). Does this suggest there were more than the twelve present? Jesus then went to Gethsemane 'accompanied by his disciples'. There a young man fled leaving his loin cloth in the hands of a soldier. Tradition names this young man as Mark himself. Was he present at the Last Supper?

In Luke we are told the apostles were at table. Jesus, taking the bread broke it and said: 'This is my body, which is given for you. Do this in memory of me' (Lk. 22:19 GNB). It is argued that the phrase 'This is my body, which is given for you' cannot possibly refer to the twelve only; therefore, to whom is Jesus making the request: 'Do this in memory of me'? As the Passover meal was the one occasion on which the entire household, men, women and children ate together, some believe the command was given not just to the twelve but to the entire community.

A similar puzzlement is caused when the two disciples at Emmaus recognised the Risen Christ in the 'breaking of the bread' and returned to Jerusalem where they found the eleven gathered together with *others*. There, while reporting their encounter, Jesus appeared in their midst and reminded them that the Scriptures had foretold that the Messiah would suffer. Then he added, 'You are witnesses of these things. And behold, I send the promise of my Father upon you; but stay in the city, until you are clothed with power from on high' (Lk. 24:48–49 RSV). Is Jesus speaking here to the eleven or to all who were gathered with them?

When Mary of Magdala went to where the *disciples* were gathered she told them she had seen the Lord. That evening Jesus appeared among them. '. . . he breathed on them, and said to them, "Receive the Holy Spirit. If you forgive the sins of any, they are forgiven; if you retain the sins of any, they are retained"' (Jn 20:22–23 RSV). Again it is asked, to whom is Jesus entrusting this power? Is it to the eleven or to all the disciples present? The passage goes on to say that one of the twelve, Thomas, was not with them when Jesus came. Does this mean that Thomas did not receive the power to forgive sins? These are some of the passages whose traditional interpretations are at present being questioned.

The Church in Jerusalem

The first Christian community, sometimes referred to as the mother Church, was based in Jerusalem. It consisted of Jews who had become followers of Jesus, some in fact were Jewish priests (Acts 6:7). These converts continued to regard themselves as practising Jews. All the faithful remained in close fellowship, sharing their belongings one with the other. Together they joined daily in the Temple worship, broke bread in each other's houses, sharing with gladness and generosity. Each day the Lord added to their number those who were being saved (Acts 2:44–47). Note that the first Christians continued to participate in the Temple rituals.

Alas, such harmony did not endure. This community consisted of local Jews who spoke Aramaic and of Jews who had lived abroad and were now Greek-speaking. Complaints were made that the widows of the returned emigrants were not receiving a fair share during the daily distribution of alms. So the twelve called the community together and asked that seven men be chosen to take over the administration of funds, thus leaving the twelve free to preach. Traditionally these seven are called deacons, but nowhere in the text is such a title used (Acts 6:1–6). Nor was their work confined to administration, for we are told immediately that one of them, Stephen, was accused of preaching against the law. Later we hear of another, Philip, 'preaching the Good News in every town' (Acts 8:40 GNB).

Peter continued as a travelling preacher while James, the brother of the Lord, emerges in the records as the leader of the Jerusalem Church. Some commentators observe that the family of Jesus did not openly support him until after his death and resurrection. The model of leadership in the Jerusalem community seems to have been that of the synagogue which had a leader and a council of elders. Decades later these Jewish Christians were still faithful to the Temple observances. Luke records Paul's eagerness to be in Jerusalem on the day of Pentecost (Acts 20:16).

On arriving back from his last missionary journey Paul went to Jerusalem as usual to report to James and the elders. There it was pointed out to him that members of the community were distressed when they heard that he had told Jewish converts living in Gentile lands that it was no longer necessary to circumcise their sons – thus forsaking the law of Moses. They advised him to join four men who had taken a vow and to pay their purification expenses; thus all would know that Paul was still faithful to Jewish practice. Next day Paul was purified with the men and 'went into the Temple and gave notice of how many days it would be until the end of the period of purification, when a sacrifice would be offered for each one of them' (Acts 21:26 GNB). This passage suggests that almost thirty years after the death and resurrection of Jesus the Christian community in Jerusalem still sought the services of Jewish priests.

It is argued that these first Christians saw themselves as a group within Judaism. Others wonder if living so close to the Temple they sought to protect themselves from further persecution. Yet when the Romans destroyed the Temple in AD70, this first Christian community dispersed. Gone was the 'mother Church' of Christianity. Gone also was the only structure Jesus ever initiated, the twelve.

A Community of Equals

Jesus had taught over and over again that no member of his movement was to lord it over others. He said, 'You know that among the Gentiles those who rule lord it over others, vaunt their power over them. With you it must be different, whoever wants to be in charge must be your servant' (Mt. 20:25–26). Elsewhere he condemned the use of status titles, and the wearing in public of elaborate religious symbols and dress (Mt. 23:5–7). While at table with his disciples on the night before he died, he rose, filled a basin with water and washed his disciples' feet. When he was again seated at table he said, 'I have washed your feet, I who am your lord and master, you in turn must wash each other's feet. I have set you an example so that you will do what I have done' (Jn 13:4–17). Some women wonder why the 'washing of the feet' has not become a sacramental ritual in the Church. Paul grasped the vision of the status-free community envisaged by Jesus and expressed it like this: 'You were baptised into oneness in Christ, and have put on Christ himself. So there is no more Jew or Gentile, slave or free, male or female, you have become one in Christ Jesus' (Gal. 3:27–28).

While the Christian community in Jerusalem remained attached to the Temple, further afield the Christian churches were developing differently. The first disciples had expected Jesus to return within their lifetime, so the emphasis was on preaching the Good News and community care. The Church in Antioch of Syria became a centre for a wider missionary activity. It was this community which sent Paul and Barnabas on their journeys and later we learn that Peter was resident there. The Church in Antioch consisted of convert Gentiles and Jews forming a community together, and it was here that the disciples were first called Christians. It was a charismatic community, that is one in which the gifts of all were acknowledged and used.

There is no evidence that these early Christians regarded any of their members as a priest in the Jewish sense of a mediator between God and the people. According to Paul each one was baptised into ministry, some as apostles or prophets, others as teachers or healers, and some had the 'gift of tongues' (1 Cor. 12:12–27). Some of the disciples had the gift of proclaiming the Good News, some were called to serve or to encourage others. Yet others had riches to share, and there were those gifted with compassionate hearts. No ministry carried status, all were for service. They were a Church of the baptised, not of the ordained. It is clear from reading Acts and the Letters that ministry did not develop around the Eucharist and liturgy. There seems to have been no problem about who presided at the 'breaking of the bread'. There is no mention of an apostle presiding, nor do any of these documents refer to anyone as priest. Both in Judaism and the Greco-Roman religions priesthood was a cultic office. For the first Christians the community collectively represented Christ, women and children included. There was no division between minister and laity as all were ministers. Each ministry was concerned with community-building and developed around proclaiming the Good News for the salvation of the world.

Both Peter and Paul are believed to have been martyred in Rome in AD64 during Nero's persecution of the Christians. It was the custom for Christian Jews to attend synagogue on the Saturday and then to observe a vigil throughout the night in the hope that Jesus would return. When he did not return they brought the vigil to a conclusion with the celebration of the Eucharist. The Roman authorities exempted Jews from offering incense to the Greco-

Roman gods. Wherever Christians were understood to be a sect within Judaism they too enjoyed this exemption. However, the night vigils were regarded with suspicion because rumour had it that the Christians claimed to eat the body and drink the blood of a man named Jesus whom they said had died but had risen again. This led to wild stories about the Christians; when they did not participate in the worship of the local gods they were labelled atheists, and whenever a natural calamity occurred the Christians were believed to have angered the gods and so were persecuted. In time they became a danger to the Jewish communities and were eventually expelled from the synagogues.

Early Structures and Organisation

The Christians of the second generation were left without Jewish support. The eye witnesses, those who had known Jesus, were dead and still Jesus had not returned. It was now the responsibility of the Church leaders to record and consolidate the teachings of Jesus for the generations yet to come. The unstructured charismatic days were over.

Paul's letters had, of course, been written during his lifetime, that is before AD64. They are the Letters to the Romans, 1 and 2 Corinthians, 1 Thessalonians, Galatians, Philippians, and Philemon. The Letters whose authorship is questioned and those believed to have been written after Paul's death are 2 Thessalonians, Colossians, Ephesians, Titus, 1 and 2 Timothy , and Hebrews. Let us be clear, the authority of these Letters is not questioned; they form part of the canon of Scripture. What *is* questioned is their authorship and the date at which they were written, for this affects the context in which they should be interpreted. It is understood that they were written by the disciples of Paul and within the Churches he established. It was the custom at that time for disciples to attribute their works to their teachers.

Paul never mentions the priesthood of Jesus. It is first mentioned in the Letter to the Hebrews (author unknown). It was written ten to twenty years after the destruction of the Temple and the author seeks to show that the sacrifice of Jesus has replaced that of the Temple. John's Gospel and Letters also date from the end of the first century and record the faith as understood by the Christians of Asia Minor. Here the Holy Spirit is seen as their leader, '. . . the Helper, the Holy Spirit, whom the Father will send in my name, will teach you everything' (Jn 14:26 GNB). 'As long as his Spirit remains in you, you do not need anyone to teach you'

(1 Jn 2:27 GNB). We are given a description of a community of equals, although John himself is referred to as an elder.

The Pastoral Epistles (1 and 2 Timothy , and Titus) introduce us to the communities of the second century. Here the Churches described are far more organised and structured than any we have met so far. These Epistles are sometimes called manuals for Church administration. The man who aspires to be leader of a Church must be without fault, faithful to one wife, sober, self-controlled, orderly, hospitable and be able to teach. He must not be a drunkard, or given to fighting, but must be polite and not be a money grabber. He should be able to manage his household and win the trust of his children. A man who is unable to order his own family will not be capable of caring for God's household (1 Tim. 3:1–5).

In 1 Timothy 5:17 it is recommended that teachers and preachers be given double pay. This is an interesting development as Paul on his last journey reminded a group of elders: 'I have taken neither silver, gold or clothing from anyone. With my hands [Paul was a tent maker] I have provided for my own needs and those of my companions' (Acts 20: 33–34).

The Greek terms *diakonos, episkcopus* and *presbyteros* are difficult to define. At times all three titles are applied to the same person. They are also applied to disciples carrying out any of a variety of ministries. However, we are warned by scholars that it would be false to try and read into these terms our present hierarchical structure of bishop, priest and deacon. Yet it is obvious from the three Pastoral Epistles that the structure of the Greco-Roman family with all its household codes, ranks and centralised authority had become the Christian model for the 'household of God'. Gone is Paul's analogy of the one body with each function of equal importance. Also gone is the discipleship of equals as envisaged by Jesus.

THE FIRST MILLENNIUM

After the Temple was destroyed the Christians began to regard themselves as the new Israel. They appropriated the Temple language and their ministers were identified with the priestly role and liturgical responsibilities.

Ignatius of Antioch, who was martyred in AD107 wrote to the Church in Smyrna exhorting the Christians there not to celebrate the Eucharist unless the *Episkopos* or one appointed by him was presiding. He asked them to obey the presbyters as they would the apostles. Thus, early in the second century we find structures and regulations introduced. Yet in the *Shepherd of Hermas* written around AD145 we learn that prophets are still functioning in Rome. Irenaeus who lived in the same century held that those in Episcopal ministry were the successors of the apostles and that deacons participated in the order of priesthood. Before he died around AD225 Tertullian advised communities in which there were no presbyters, to baptise and to celebrate the Eucharist themselves, saying, 'You are your own priests and where two or three are gathered there is the Church.' So until the middle of the second century there was still no universal structure throughout the Christian community.

The Mandate of the People

During the third century books of rituals began to appear. The most important of these is the *Apostolic Traditions* of Hippolitus of Rome written about AD230. It states that authority rests in the community and that no episcopus, presbyter or deacon may be ordained unless first requested by the community that is willing to accept their ministry. Ordination is referred to as sacramental and is related to the Eucharist. It goes on to say that it is the role of the episcopus 'to feed his flock'. This is in line with the command given by Jesus to Peter. There is no directive to rule. Any connection between ordination and jurisdiction was as yet unthinkable in these communities. A minister who became ill or misbehaved was relieved of his ministry.

Cyprian, Bishop of Carthage, insisted that no bishop should be imposed upon the people, they were to choose whoever they wanted. He did not regard ordination as permanent, believing the people had a right to depose an unworthy bishop. None of the Fathers of the Church promoted priesthood as a separate caste with power over the community. Cyprian did however associate ordination with Eucharist and used Jewish sacrificial terminology.

Rome the First Among Equals

Cyprian held that baptism administered outside the Spirit-led community was null and void. Stephen, Bishop of Rome from AD254–255, disagreed saying the sacrament did not belong to the Church but to Christ and therefore could be administered by anyone anywhere. The debate became so heated that Stephen invoked the Scripture passage: 'Thou art Peter and upon this rock I will build my Church. . . . To you I give the keys of the kingdom'

(Mt. 16:18–19) and claimed that as the successor of Peter the greater authority rested with him. This is the first record we have of a Bishop of Rome appealing to this Matthean text in order to claim primacy. Cyprian, however, did not accept this interpretation, insisting that all bishops held equal authority and were answerable only to God and their communities.[1]

The authority of Rome continued to be the subject of keen debate until the end of the third century when it was accepted by both the Eastern and Western Churches that the Bishop of Rome was for the whole Church the 'first among equals' and 'the centre of unity'. This agreement did not lead to centralised government. The local churches continued to be grouped around the four main Patriarchates of Jerusalem, Antioch, Alexandria and Rome.

A Two-Tiered Church

In AD313 the Emperor Constantine legalised the Christian religion and Church leaders were now accorded the same privileges and status as the State priests. They were exempted from military service and given places of honour at the Roman festivals. Thus without consultation or debate Christians found themselves with a two-tiered Church and the seeds of clericalism were sown. In AD381 the Emperor Theodosius established Christianity as the state religion of the Roman Empire and the Church entered into what many consider its sad unholy history as a secular power.

Jesus had instituted the Eucharist within the Passover meal, which was a family ritual presided over by a family elder, not by a priest. But as the model of the Jewish cultic priesthood developed in the Church the power to consecrate was focused on the person of the priest rather than on the priestly people until gradually the priest came to be perceived as the dispenser of sacramental grace.

During the first century ministry had been associated with proclaiming the Good News, teaching and community care. It was not associated with the carrying out of ritual or presiding at the Eucharist. Even in the early second century the job descriptions for ministers given in Timothy and Titus had no reference to liturgical duties. By the fifth century, however, church life was centred around the Patriarchs, with resident bishops in each local church who were said to have succeeded collectively to the role of the twelve. By now the terms 'apostle' and 'prophet' had disappeared from the records.

The Council of Chalcedon met in AD451 and canon 6 directed that: 'No man may be ordained in a vacuum, but only after being assigned to a community in city, country, martyr's shrine or monastery. The laying on of hands on any man for whom the community has not asked is null and void.' Meanwhile in the East the Bishops of Constantinople, Carthage and Caesarea had become Patriarchs and each Patriarchy remained independent though still recognising the Patriarch of Rome as the 'centre of unity' and 'first among equals'. Eventually the Patriarchs took upon themselves the right to appoint bishops 'after consultation with the people'. Then as the Empire began to decline even the local bishops were obliged to undertake more and more civil duties and offices, so that, by the end of the fifth century the Church which had begun as a network of small house communities had developed into a powerful organisation presided over by monarch-like Patriarchs and bishops.

When Attila the Hun invaded Italy Pope Leo I bravely went out to meet him and through the process of negotiation managed to save Rome. Twenty years later in AD476 the Empire in the West collapsed. In the East the Empire continued for many more centuries ruled over from Constantinople. By AD756 Pepin III, King of the Franks, had donated Rome itself and other large tracts of land to Pope Stephen II. This territory became known as the Papal States and was added to by succeeding popes. As the secular power of the papacy increased bishops looked to the pope for protection from their local rulers and so in time they became more and more dependent on Rome.

A Sacrificial Priesthood

By the eighth century the sacrificial aspect of the Eucharist was emphasised and the bishops and presbyters were regarded as priest-mediators. The faithful became those who were ministered to. There is now mention of the anointing of the priest's hands so as to bestow on him the power to consecrate. During the celebration of the Eucharist the priest offered the prayers in silence on behalf of a silenced community and choirs were introduced to provide the singing.

This same century also saw the introduction of the daily private Mass. This development was never accepted in the Eastern Churches which restrict the celebration of the Eucharist to Sundays and feast days. With the daily Mass abuses crept in. Monks were ordained to offer Masses solely for the dead, some offered up to twelve Masses a day without any congregation present. Votive Masses for special intentions were then sought and the monks were kept busier than ever. The Eucharist became the property of the clergy. By the ninth century the bread was replaced with a wafer and the chalice was no longer given to the people. The Body of Christ which for centuries was understood to mean the Christian community now came to mean the consecrated host.

Jesus never sought civil power. His mission was to preach the Good News, to challenge the religious and civil authorities, and to call all to repentance. By the close of the first millennium those who called themselves 'the Vicar of Christ on Earth' had formed armies to protect their vast civil power and wealth.

The Second Millennium

At the beginning of the second millennium Christian religious practice had reached an all-time low. The feudal system had produced Prince Bishops. The priesthood had become the personal status of the individual. There was a shift from ministry and community to private Masses. Only monks, nuns and priests received Communion regularly. The laity simply saw the sacred host raised at the consecration. A bell was rung to mark the moment. On a Sunday many of the devout hurried from church to church to be present at the moment of the elevation. This gave rise to new devotions, including Benediction, a semi-liturgical celebration that aimed at prolonging the elevation period[2] and Corpus Christi processions during which the priest carried the host in a gold monstrance through the town.

In 1074 Pope Gregory VII set about introducing some reforms. He tried to abolish simony (the buying or selling of spiritual privileges) and to enforce celibacy among the clergy. But his main aim was to free the Church from the control of the civil rulers who had begun to install popes and bishops of their own choice.

Discontent grew among the people and they began to ask questions. First they wanted to know how grace was transmitted in the Church, then they sought to have the primacy of the pope clarified, and the canon lawyers were anxious to distinguish between spiritual powers and jurisdiction. Until the twelfth century both the Orthodox and Latin Churches had accepted that when a priest ceased to serve the community he returned to the lay state, but the idea of a permanent priesthood was gaining support in some quarters. As the discontent spread the people set about forming lay associations.

In 1232 the Emperor Frederick II issued an edict against heretics and in response Pope Gregory IX established the

Inquisition. The lay associations were suppressed. During the next three centuries millions of women were either burned or executed as witches by the officers of the Inquisition. To kill them was to cleanse the Body of Christ. These were the women who did not fit into patriarchy. They were spinsters or widows acting as healers and mid-wives, independent women who inspired trust in women and suspicion in men.

Despite the persecutions many committed lay Christians continued to protest at the wealth, pomp and general lifestyle of some of the bishops. They also questioned the sacramental system as controlled by the clergy and decided to rely more on the Gospel promises concerning the Spirit at work within themselves.

Reformation and Counter-Reformation

The swell of discontent within the Roman Catholic Church finally reached bursting point when in 1517 Martin Luther, an Augustinian priest and lecturer at the university of Wittenburg, condemned the practice of selling indulgences and proclaimed the priesthood of the people based on baptism. He turned away from the numerous devotions supported by Church officials and aimed to return the Bible to the people. Around the same time John Calvin, a French theologian living in Geneva, preached that Jesus was the sole mediator. He outlined a programme for ministry which omitted any mention of priesthood and said he could not identify the sixteenth-century Church structures with Scripture teachings. The Scandinavian, German, Swiss, English and Hungarian rulers gradually withdrew their allegiance to Rome and established their own national Churches.

The Roman response was to call a Council at Trent in 1545 which met over three sessions until 1563. All Councils meet within a historical context and are concerned with current needs. Rome was not prepared for the challenge of the Reformation and so simply concentrated on those issues raised by the reformers. Those attending the council endeavoured to rebut the emphasis placed on the return to first-century Church practice. The papal theologians themselves also studied the Scripture sources and argued that Jesus had instituted the sacramental priesthood through the apostles. The hierarchical structure of bishop, priest, deacon and faithful was said to be of divine law and that God had allowed these distinctions to develop.

Jurisdiction proved to be an issue causing considerable tension. Some bishops believed their authority came direct from God, while others accepted that it was given to them by the Bishop of Rome. To prevent the nobles from continuing to interfere in ecclesiastical appointments it was decided to exclude the laity entirely and to allow only members of the clergy to submit nominations for Episcopal appointments.

The reformers had objected to the celebrations of the Eucharist without the participation of the community. They translated the Bible into the local languages so as to enable the people to study the Scriptures for themselves. Trent, on the other hand, stressed the importance of the sacraments and directed that they be made central to the future spiritual formation of both the clergy and laity. Attendance at daily Mass and the frequent confession of sins were encouraged. The Forty Hours Adoration and devotional visits to the Blessed Sacrament reserved in the churches was an outcome of this new formation. Trent decreed that at solemn high Masses only the priest was to receive Holy Communion, so for many Catholics it became the norm to offer the Mass without participating in Communion. No arrangement was made to translate the Bible so that the majority of Catholics remained spiritually dependent on the clergy.

The First Vatican Council

By the nineteenth century Rome had so extended its network of nunciatures and Curia departments that it was possible to monitor the activities of the local churches. When in 1868 the pope called the First Vatican Council a large number of Church leaders, who favoured an even more centralised authority administered by the Curia, moved to have papal infallibility defined. Another group of bishops stood out for diocesan independence and sought to have the infallibility of the whole Church defined first.

However, during the Council it was the question of papal infallibility that was dealt with. It was restricted to those formal statements made *ex cathedra* by the pope on matters of faith and morals. Then before the Spirit's infallible guidance of the whole Church could be discussed war broke out between France and Prussia. The Piedmontese armies took advantage of the upheaval, invaded the Papal States and captured Rome. The Council Fathers fled, leaving behind them a lot of unfinished business.

By the end of the war the Papal States were gone and the pope was confined to the mini-Vatican State inside Rome. In 1889 a new catechism was issued which stated that the Bishop of Rome as Vicar of Christ on earth and successor of Peter was infallible when preaching *ex cathedra* on matters of faith and morals. During the next century three generations of Catholics were taught this one aspect of the doctrine of infallibility.

The Second Vatican Council

Then it all happened. In 1958 John XXIII became Pope. He declared that he was about to open windows and proceeded to lead the Latin Church out of four hundred years of entrenchment during which it had resisted outside influences. He opened the Second Vatican Council in 1962 and directed it to continue where the last Council had broken off. Infallibility as it related to the pope was reaffirmed but extended to include all the bishops when they were united on a teaching, especially when meeting in Council. Vatican II accepted some of what the sixteenth-century reformers had sought. The liturgy was translated into the vernacular, the priesthood of the people was stressed, and Catholics were encouraged to study their Jewish roots.

It fell to Paul VI to implement the decrees of Vatican II. He restored the permanent diaconate especially for married men and in so doing separated the link between ordination and the Eucharist. The deacon is mandated to preach, preside at marriages and funerals, and to carry out other pastoral functions. It is now thirty years since the documents of Vatican II were published. Younger students regard them as part of ancient history. With many of the decrees still waiting to be put into practice the Council seems to have little relevance for many of today's Catholics.

Clericalism

In recent years the word 'clericalism' has been used to sum up a disconcerting attitude observed in the clerical culture surrounding the Christian priesthood. Clericalism has been described as an elitist caste system that operates in a power-over mode towards the faithful. When challenged it goes on the defensive, anxious to present an aura of sacredness. It is a mentality that can eventually isolate and dehumanise the priest. Colm Kilcoyne, priest and journalist writing in an Irish newspaper, defined clericalism as a control system that feeds off its sense of God-given superiority; he said that it rewards servility and punishes independence no matter how loyal, and added that it has its own lay associate membership. He believes the time has come for a hierarchy that has condemned materialism, secularism and individualism to now condemn clericalism.[3] Andrew Oyalana of the Department of Religious

Studies in the University of Ilorin, Nigeria, holds that 'secularism is a critique, not so much of religion as of the massive abuse of powers by the Churches'. He accuses Church leaders of having infantilised people and says 'the opposite of secular is by no means religious, but ecclesiastic'.[4]

The 1990 Synod on 'The Formation of Priests' re-emphasised the programme devised at Trent. This upset many women who believe that priests already talk only from their heads and their text books. They suggest that all priestly formation should include work with the mentally handicapped for whom abstract thought has little relevance. It is also suggested that seminarians continue to live among the people during their years of training and that they attend personal development courses. But most of all it is seen as essential that seminaries open their study halls to women, not only to ensure that our future priests are taught by women scholars but that they have women students sharing with them in their class discussions. At the 1996 meeting of the National Council of Priests of England and Wales it was pointed out that not only was the priest set apart but so was the seminarian. Many of the priests present complained that they felt trapped by the expectations of their role.[5]

Any change aimed at bringing about a declericalisation of ministry has to affect not only those who exercise authority but also those who are denied it. Priests trained for the traditional model of priesthood will at times feel bewildered, even disillusioned, as the old securities of the role disappear and they experience new and unfamiliar responses from the people. The process has already begun for many priests. On the other hand, wherever the laity have been trained into respectful passivity it will take much more confidence building to enable them to undertake their responsibility for ministry.

There are two simple changes that could help to alter attitudes.

1. Drop the title 'Father' as conferred on Catholic priests. It was introduced less than two hundred years ago and is forbidden by the Gospels (Mt. 23:9). It leads to paternalism and today becomes the butt of crude comments. The term 'minister' has been suggested but some people would prefer to use the term 'brother'.
2. Use inclusive language, especially in the liturgy, wherever the local language is sexist – for example: the English language is sexist, the Irish language is not.

Priests who have studied the new Christian feminist insights often find themselves going through the whole bereavement process of denial, anger, bargaining, depression, guilt and finally acceptance. Once the alternative vision is glimpsed and recognised as Gospel-based there is no return to the old mind-sets.

Vatican II presents the Church as there for the sake of the world. Therefore the needs of the world have to set the agenda. Many committed Christians wonder why we talk of a vocation crisis. Ministry is not the preserve of the ordained. Instead of praying for an increase in priestly and religious vocations it might be more Gospel-like to pray for the building up of Christian communities in which all minister according to their gifts.

> The Spirit's gifts are present to each one for the good of all.
> (1 Cor. 12:7)

PAUSE FOR REFLECTION

1. How would the active ministry for all the baptised, if put into practice, affect your community?
2. Would you favour a change in the celibacy rule for priests? Why?

5

Religious life and its Ever-Changing Forms

At first thought many people would presume that nuns, above all women, were respected and honoured by the priestly leadership of the Church. However, even a brief look at history will show how deeply rooted was the male distrust of the female.

World Religions and Religious Life

Religious life is not the monopoly of the Roman Catholic Church. Religious life existed thousands of years before Christ, and it continues to thrive within Hinduism and Buddhism. In these oriental monasteries and convents some of the nuns and monks live out their entire lives, but the majority enter for a specific number of years, usually during their youth. They receive training in spirituality and self-discipline, then leave to fulfil their 'duty to society' by working in a trade or profession, marrying and rearing a family. As they grow older some again withdraw from secular life.

Religious life did not develop within Judaism. There are records of a first-century community called the Essenes, which was based in the desert near the Dead Sea. The members did not approve of the Temple leadership in Jerusalem. Some scholars suggest that John the Baptist may have belonged to this community and that Jesus may have stayed with the Essenes whenever he withdrew into the desert.

It took four hundred years before the first signs of religious life appeared within Christianity. Today it is accepted as a way of life by the Orthodox, Roman Catholic and Anglo-Catholic Churches. The Reformed Churches did not consider it a lifestyle in keeping with the Gospels, though there are now a few Lutheran convents. Nor is the religious life found within Islam. Perhaps the nearest approximation to it would be found in the Sufi ascetical tradition.

By the second century the Church had devised a ritual for the consecration of virgins and widows called to the public service of the community. However, they were not religious and continued to live in their family homes.

THE FIRST MILLENNIUM

In AD313 the Roman Emperor Constantine legalised the Christian religion. Hitherto, Christians had been subject to sporadic persecutions and so only those with a deep commitment to Christ remained faithful. Later, when Constantine was baptised it became fashionable to join the new religion. On witnessing the wealth and self-indulgence of many of these converts, some Christian men and women withdrew into the deserts to lead lives of prayer and fasting. They became counter-signs to the prevailing culture. Young men and women who became disciples of these first hermits were gradually formed into organised communities. Around 360 Basil, a hermit who later became bishop in Cappadocia, wrote a rule of life which to this day has remained a guide for Eastern monasticism.

With the fall of the Roman Empire in 476 Europe was plunged into chaos. By 500 the young Benedict of Nursia felt called to leave the lawlessness of Roman society and with like-minded companions set up twelve monasteries, the most famous of which was that at Monte Cassino. His twin sister, Scholastica, founded similar communities of women. These monks and nuns vowed to live lives of stability and so in their turn became a counter-sign within the prevailing social unrest. Their convents and monasteries were oases of learning and hospitality, where students were instructed, the sick nursed, and travellers provided with a safe refuge.

Meanwhile, in the Celtic lands bordering Western Europe, the Church was centred almost entirely within the monastic settlements, while the bishops acted as priest-chaplains to the wider Christian community. Back on mainland Europe a similar development was taking place with over seventeen thousand abbeys and priories established by the eighth century. So, from being secluded havens of prayer and learning, the monasteries became the centres of Church influence and political power, ruled over by prince abbots. These monasteries amassed enormous wealth and were organised along feudal lines with the manual work provided by serfs who lived on the monastery lands.

The Second Millennium

By the end of the tenth century the monks in the monastery at Cluny had reintroduced the original rule of Benedict. Gradually the reform was taken up by other monasteries and by the eleventh century they became centralised under Cluny. Some scholars mark the beginning of the religious orders from this period.

In 1209 Francis of Assisi, son of a wealthy merchant, gave his disciples a rule of life based on sayings from the Gospels. He emphasised absolute poverty, not only for the individual disciples whom he called friars or brothers, but for the community as a whole. Again we see God raising up within the Church a group of people who became a counter-sign to their contemporaries. It was Francis' insistence on poverty that delayed papal approval for his new order. Pope Innocent III and the Bishop of Assisi both felt threatened by the poverty proposed by Francis, declaring that it was not in accordance with the Scriptures. Finally he got approval but refused to take a vow of stability. He argued that the friars were called to take the Gospel message from village to village to those who, intimidated by the grandeur, failed to attend the monastic services. By the end of the thirteenth century there were several thousand Franciscan friars evangelising the poor in Europe.

Around 1215 Francis accepted Clare, a young noblewoman of Assisi, as a disciple and installed her with some companions in the convent of San Damiano. An itinerant lifestyle was of the essence of the Franciscan missionary calling, but perhaps because of pressure from the authorities Francis – unlike Jesus – refused to have women companions on his journeys. Instead, strict enclosure was imposed on Clare and her companions. In 1219 when Francis was about to set out for the Middle East to preach to the Saracens, Clare asked to accompany him but was firmly refused. The nuns were told that their calling was to pray for the work of the friars. A recently discovered document shows that Clare had understood the Gospel vision of 'a discipleship of equals'; she had wished to exercise a communal leadership, but this was not acceptable to the Church authorities who appointed her as abbess in 1215 and so confirmed a hierarchical structure on her community.

During this same century the Albigensians were busy preaching that Jesus was not truly human, but was an angel in disguise and therefore had not really died. They rejected the body as evil, discouraged marriage and led very strict lives. Francis was never ordained, but now in 1216 a young Spanish priest named Dominic received papal approval for his Order of Preachers. Like Francis he called his companions friars and they too travelled abroad. They were committed to stamping out the Albigensian heresy in Europe by means of writing, preaching and lecturing. Dominic also founded enclosed communities of women. Oddly enough, to this day the Dominican Sisters officially place the letters OP (Order of Preachers) after their names, but being women are forbidden by the Church authorities to preach.

In 1534 the Spanish soldier Ignatius of Loyola founded the Society of Jesus whose members became known as the Jesuits. They gave special emphasis to the vow of obedience and held themselves free to be sent wherever they were most needed. Ignatius and his companions offered their services to the pope and were entrusted with the task of spearheading the Counter-Reformation. This they did by educating Catholics and by preaching to non-Christian peoples. They avoided monastic structures, did not pray the divine office in common and their leaders were appointed for a limited period. During his lifetime Ignatius sent his companions to Brazil, China, Ethiopia, India, Japan, Zaire, and all over Europe. Thus the Church saw the start of the modern apostolic missionary orders that continued to be founded, as needs arose, right into the twentieth century.

The Effects of Patriarchy on Women Religious

Enclosure

> Jesus travelled from town to village preaching the Good News of God's Kingdom. With him travelled the twelve disciples and certain women who had been freed from evil spirits and other illnesses. (Lk. 8:1–2)

Jesus broke with local customs and invited women to travel with him on his missionary journeys. Yet nowhere in the Gospels is there any record of the religious authorities or the people using this fact to accuse Jesus and his companions of improper behaviour.

As we have seen, a thousand years later when Clare wished to accompany Francis on his mission to the Saracens she was refused and obliged to exercise her ministry from behind the convent grille. These grilles have been compared to the chastity belts into which the crusaders locked their wives, because women were considered too weak to resist temptation. The enclosed convents were called tombs and the nuns said to be entombed with Christ. In Spain under the Islamic influence they were known as 'mystical harems'. Pope Boniface VIII in 1298 made enclosure compulsory for all women religious. Three centuries later nuns were required to take solemn vows.

In 1535, a year after Ignatius founded his society of apostolic religious, Angela Merici founded an association of women in northern Italy under the patronage of Saint Ursula. They were committed to the work of education, but instead of opening schools they decided to support family life by teaching the children at home. Angela Merici had no thought of taking solemn vows or of wearing a distinctive dress. She and her companions understood their call to service as rooted in their baptism commitment. However, the Church authorities demanded that she observe 'the canonical safeguards required of nuns' if they were to continue to teach the children.

Mary Ward was born into the England of the penal laws when English Catholics had to learn to live without priest or sacrament. Her grandmother and her aunt both spent many years in prison refusing to deny their allegiance to the Holy See. Thus, early in life Mary saw first-hand the strength of women in the Church. To meet an obvious need she gathered together a group of courageous women who in secret taught children the 'old faith', reconciled those who had denied the Roman Church, and attended to the dying. Her work spread to the continent where she opened convents and schools. She called her community The Institute of the Blessed Virgin Mary, but because of their lifestyle the sisters were soon dubbed 'Jesuitesses'. From her experience in England Mary realised that she had no need of the traditional regulations imposed on women religious (i.e. the enclosure, the habit, or the recitation of the divine office in common) but the prevailing attitude to women in the Church prevented the acceptance of her evident good work. She was accused of leading her companions into grave moral danger.

Twenty years after she had started her work Urban VIII, though believing in Mary's sincerity, came to regard the type of institute she had founded as a 'poisonous growth in the Church of God' that needed to be rooted out. He insisted that enclosure was necessary to protect the sisters from their moral and intellectual weaknesses. In 1631 he ordered Mary to close down her convents and schools. Some of the sisters entered enclosed convents, some returned to their families, while a few continued loyal to Mary's ideals. Mary was imprisoned as a 'rebel to Holy Church' and denied the sacraments unless she admitted the errors of her ways. When a cleric confessed he 'would not for a thousand worlds be a woman because women are incapable of a relationship with God', Mary commented: 'I could have told him of the experience I have to the contrary, but I desisted and only smiled; I could have pitied his lack of judgment. But no, I'm wrong; he is a man of very good judgment, his lack is in experience!'

Two years after the suppression of Mary Ward's foundations Vincent de Paul founded with Louise de Marillac in 1633 an organisation of women which he named the Daughters of Charity. The need was for the sick poor in Paris to be cared for in their homes. Here he faced a dilemma. To avoid the restrictions placed on consecrated women, Vincent arranged for the Daughters of Charity to make a yearly commitment instead of perpetual vows. As they went about their work he advised them to 'let the streets be your cloister'.

By 1775 the heiress Nano Nagle had opened seven schools for the children of the poor in her native city of Cork. Wishing to have a stable teaching staff, she arranged for some Ursulines to come from the continent to Ireland, but as they were bound by enclosure they could only take over the management of one school based within their convent. This left Nano with six schools to staff and maintain. She and her companions continued to teach in the schools and to nurse the sick in their homes. However, after her death the sight of a group of dedicated women 'out and about' was unacceptable to the Irish Church and so these women, known as the Presentation Sisters, were formally enclosed.

Not long after this Catherine McAuley in 1827 opened her first house in Baggot Street, Dublin. It was a day school for poor children and a night hostel for girls in domestic service. The house was placed under the patronage of Our Lady of Mercy. Daughters of the wealthy business and professional classes joined Catherine in her work. Some took up residence with her and there, in the House of Mercy, they lived as a community. Though this house was opened with the permission of the archbishop he later decided that if the work was to continue Catherine and her companions would have to become religious or leave the house and allow women religious to manage it. Catherine had never before considered becoming a religious, but now at the age of fifty-two she undertook a two-year noviciate under the direction of the Presentation Sisters. In 1835 the Congregation of the Sisters of Mercy was canonically approved by Gregory XVI. These are just a few of the women who, inspired by God to meet the needs of their time, were curtailed in their ministries by the un-Christlike attitudes towards women prevalent not only in society but also in the Church.

The Religious Habit

> Jesus said: Be on your guard against the teachers of the Law, who enjoy walking about in long robes and being treated with deference in the market place. (Mk 12:38)
>
> On the night before he died Jesus said: the sign by which people will know that you are my disciples is by the love you show one to the other. (Jn 13:35)

By the second century a public ceremony of veiling had been introduced for the consecration of virgins. During the next century, Tertullian directed all women to wear veils, mothers for the sake of their sons, sisters for the sake of their brothers, daughters for the sake of their fathers, as they faced dangers at every age. When Basil was visiting the hermits of Egypt in the fourth century he decided that a distinctive dress would prove 'an effective instrument to enable a monk realise his station and keep him from indecorous conduct', and so the habit as a controlling mechanism was introduced.

In the West monks did not wear a distinctive dress. In fact in the fifth century Pope Celestine I complained of the distinctive dress worn by the clergy in Gaul. 'We bishops must be distinguished from the people . . . by our learning not by our dress, by our life not by our roles, by purity of heart not by elegance.' Benedict on founding his monasteries in the following century directed that the clothes worn by the monks be suitable to the climate and the local conditions.

After the Barbarian invasion, when new dress fashions were introduced, the Western clergy clung to the Roman style which became the ritual vestments of the Catholic Church. Documents from the fourth Council of Constantinople held in 870 show that the monks and nuns of the East wore a uniform dress. Gradually, the Church authorities in the West began to appreciate the disciplinary effectiveness of a uniform and so, during the thirteenth century, Pope Boniface VIII decreed that any vowed religious who failed to wear a habit was to be excommunicated.

Vincent de Paul, still determined to keep the Daughters of Charity free of canonical control, told them to let holy modesty be their veil. They wore the local peasant costume of the time but did not change with the fashions, so that over the centuries their 'butterfly' head-dress became very distinctive.

Vatican II decreed that religious habits were to be simple, modest, in keeping with health and poverty, and to be 'becoming'. By 1976 clergy and religious were free to wear clothes suitable to an occupation, e.g. work or leisure activities.

At Maynooth on 1 October 1979 Pope John Paul II pleaded with priests and religious not to 'help the trend towards "taking God off the streets" by adopting secular modes of dress and behaviour'. The Pope gave this address out of doors in the early morning. The sisters had gathered in their thousands to keep an all-night vigil of prayer and hymn singing. A woman journalist who had sat out the cold night with them, when describing the occasion on national radio, reported that the sisters were full of life and enthusiasm but made a dull show in their black, navy blue, brown and grey; then early in the morning John Paul appeared dressed in a cream soutane and wearing a magnificent red velvet cloak set off by a gold tasselled black broad-brimmed hat. She wondered how the Holy Father dared to comment on the sisters' dress.

In 1983 the Vatican Congregation for Religious stated that without a religious habit 'it is certain that religious witness is not given'. That same year the Code of Canon Law was published and laid down that the habit was to be worn as a sign of consecration (Can. 669).

For many women religious the insistence on the habit is just another aspect of the patriarchal mind, of men trying to control women, of men knowing what is best for them. But habits, like all uniforms, separate people into 'them and us', a situation more and more women religious are striving to avoid. A growing number of women's congregations have opted to use a small cross or emblem as their sign of consecration. But unless the sign, whether it be habit, cross or emblem, is understood by others it remains meaningless. A person wearing a religious dress today may be perceived by some as a member of a privileged or oppressive class, or simply as a social worker, and by others as someone who is credulous and immature. In some African markets the sight of a sister wearing a veil is a cause for jocose and bawdy remarks.

Rank and Position

Perhaps the most harmful effect of patriarchy on women religious came from the obligation to observe within their convents the class distinctions of secular society. This was totally contrary to Gospel teaching. Back in the thirteenth century Clare had tried to be rid of it but was forbidden by Church authorities.

Biographers of Teresa of Avila describe how in the sixteenth century ladies entered convents accompanied by their maids. In convents that housed unwilling members discipline and devotion broke down. After twenty years of a life of self-indulgence Teresa left her convent and at the age of forty-seven opened Carmelite convents of strict reform. Yet she retained the two ranks of choir sisters and lay sisters. While the choir sisters sang the divine office in chapel or studied spiritual books the lay sisters saw to the domestic needs of the community.

By the eighteenth century new forms of active apostolic congregations were founded and existed separately from the traditional enclosed communities. These apostolic societies were each founded to meet a particular need. The first members usually worked together under the guidance of the foundress. When they came to seek Church approval clerics were appointed to help draw up a rule of life, and it was usually at this stage that the two ranks were introduced. Occasionally the foundress was herself of the working class and had brought together working-class companions to serve the needs of the poor. These sisters, when they sought the approbation of the Church leaders, often met with resistance and found it hard to win the trust of the clergy. By the 1950s Pope Pius XII had introduced directives modifying the differences made between the ranks. With Vatican II all such differences ceased within communities of women religious.

Clarifications

There are three ranks within the ordained ministry: deacon, priest, and bishop.

Deacons

Deacons are ordained to a pastoral ministry. The permanent diaconate is conferred on those who will never go forward for priesthood. In the Catholic Church it is sometimes conferred on married men. Those ordained to the temporary diaconate are studying for the priesthood and in the Catholic Church it is at this stage that they make their promise, not a vow, of celibacy.

Priests

Priests are persons authorised to offer sacrifice. In the Latin, Orthodox and Anglican Churches the priests administer sacraments and exercise a pastoral ministry based on the example of Jesus. It is recognised that all Christians are baptised into the priesthood of Christ and so form a priestly people.

The vast majority of Roman Catholic priests are celibates as a condition of their being ordained. They make a promise of obedience to their bishop and usually minister within their own diocese, hence they are known as secular diocesan priests. The majority of Orthodox and Anglican priests are married. There are a relatively small number of married diocesan priests in the Roman Catholic Church most of whom were ordained and married in their own Church before transferring to the Roman allegiance. Priest religious are ordained within their religious congregations to carry out the particular mission of that community wherever they are sent. Occasionally they are co-opted to minister as diocesan priests.

Bishops

Bishops are ordained into the 'fullness of the priesthood'. Each local church is centred around its bishop. The person ordained Bishop of Rome is accepted as 'first among equals' and 'the centre of unity' by all the Roman Catholic bishops and the Uniates who are those Orthodox bishops in union with Rome. Orthodox bishops are usually chosen from among the Eastern monks and so are celibate. Most Anglican bishops are married.

Religious

Religious are those who make the public vows of religion and live a shared life as members of a religious community. They may be nuns, monks, hermits, priests, religious brothers or sisters. The centuries-old communities are called orders, those founded in more recent times are known as societies or institutes. In 1996 in the Dublin diocese alone there were 141 different orders and congregations, ninety-three of women, forty-eight of men. In some orders, silent and choral prayer together with manual work, both agricultural and artistic, occupy most of the day. Other communities run institutions such as hospitals, schools, colleges, homes, or day care centres. Yet others are involved in retreat work, in printing and media ministry or in caring for the poor in their homes.

Religious Brothers

Religious Brothers are met with in two types of communities. In the clerical communities that have priests and lay brothers, the latter are usually not eligible for leadership roles. Steps are being taken to change these two rank regulations. Then there are the congregations of brothers in which all are of equal rank and all train to carry out the particular mission entrusted to the community.

Vows of Religion

The vows of religion are chastity, poverty and obedience and did not become the norm for religious until the twelfth century. Some religious take a fourth vow depending on the purpose of their order. It may be a vow of stability, that is to remain within the one monastery, or a vow to be at the service of the pope, or a vow to serve the economically poor.

Religious make either solemn or simple vows. Solemn vows are those vows which the Church leaders claim they have no power to dissolve. Women religious who take solemn vows are called nuns and are usually enclosed.

Simple vows are those vows which the Church authorities can dispense. Women religious who take simple vows are religious sisters and belong to the active apostolic congregations. In popular speech religious sisters are inaccurately referred to as 'nuns'. It is interesting to note that the 1917 Code of Canon Law stressed the differences between the solemn and simple vows, while the 1983 Code, though mentioning the two types of vows, does not distinguish between them.

Celibacy

Celibacy is not an essential element of priesthood. Lately there has been a debate within the Roman Catholic Church concerning the promise of celibacy which is obligatory for diocesan priests. People have questioned the justice of this rule. In Ireland women began to phone in to the radio chat shows complaining about the constant priority given to men's needs in our 'male-ridden' Church. They demanded that the 'nuns' be allowed to marry. Of course, there is no comparison between the two situations. Religious – whether monks, nuns, priests, brothers or sisters – freely choose not to marry. Marriage and religious life are by their nature mutually exclusive.

The vow of chastity [illegible] a vow to love God alone. That is not a Gospel ideal. It is to love [illegible] neighbour in union with God, sharing in the divine love. It is to be open to friendships that are non-possessive and do not create dependency. It is to regard others with a compassionate mind. The greatest failure for a consecrated celibate is to fail to learn to love, to become self-focused and emotionally hardened. A selfish consecrated celibate is as much a misfit as is the one who seeks genital relationships.

Poverty

Poverty as the object of a vow is a cause of disquiet for some Catholics who see it as an insult to the poor. Poverty is often equated with destitution, a state not to be aspired to but to be eradicated from the earth. Jesus was brought up by trades people and was himself a carpenter so would have enjoyed a measure of economic security. Religious themselves have considered the word 'poverty' as implied in the vow and asked if an alternative title is needed today in order to convey the meaning of the vow. They have suggested a vow to live a simple lifestyle or to share all things in common, but even these titles could lead to misunderstandings. By the vow of poverty, religious give up their right to the independent use of money, entrust their personal resources to the congregation, and through their dependence on their community express their dependence on God.

The vow of poverty is about sharing, about detachment from material things, about hospitality, working with integrity, not damaging but caring for material goods. It is not about 'not possessing' but about living the Gospel vision. Francis had wanted his order to own nothing; this the Church authorities refused. Today some committed young Catholics question the common ownership of institutions, such as hospitals and schools, claiming that such ownership gives religious a controlling power over those involved in the institutions. They believe that control over others has no place in religious life and that religious should reject that kind of ownership. They would prefer religious to manage institutions on behalf of others, which in turn causes religious to ask how best to secure their obligations to participate in policy- and decision-making.

Obedience

Obedience as vowed by religious is not a flight from responsibility. This vow was the one most emphasised by the modern congregations and is linked to mission and to taking personal responsibility for seeking the will of God in one's regard. This is first sought through reflecting on the inner God-given inspirations and desires, then through observing the needs of the times and finally through consultation with the community and those entrusted with the service of authority. It requires a great inner freedom and integrity.

Young men and women who in the past entered authoritarian communities were trained to give unquestioned obedience. Since the changes brought in by Vatican II these now older religious sometimes find it difficult to express their desires, believing that in so doing they are betraying their vow. Others experience the changes as a return to common sense.

A number of religious are very conscious of the fact that the terminology used in regard to religious life sounds elitist and divisive. For example all Christians are called to live chaste lives, to avoid greed and to seek God's will. Such phrases as 'has a vocation' or 'is called' take from the whole truth. All baptised people have a vocation and have been called to participate in the mission of Christ to the world.

Renewal in Religious Life

For almost three centuries the active apostolic women's congregations had been obliged to carry out their active ministries within a monastic framework, some even within an enclosure. According to canon law women religious were minors. Some described the sisters as 'nuns let out on long leads'. They worked in public yet wore the fashions of a previous century and observed a rule of silence, speaking only when absolutely necessary. Within their convents monastic prayer patterns were followed. The divine office was chanted five times daily, and contact with seculars was limited to work obligations and a few visits from family or friends.

Vatican II relieved religious sisters of their monastic structures and gave them twelve years in which to experiment and find a life-style more suitable to their mission. But alas they were not skilled in public relations and so both clergy and people were confused by the changes. They saw sisters modify their habits, then later don modern dress as they moved out of their convents and in small groups settled into family-sized homes. The mystique rapidly vanished as the sisters were encountered as neighbours and colleagues. Some sisters unable to cope without the monastic structures joined enclosed orders, others on becoming more aware of the fundamental vocation of baptism began to regard the religious life as too elitist and decided to leave.

New religious congregations are always founded to meet a particular need, usually on the margins of society, and there signal to both the Church and society the urgency of an alternative approach to current injustices. Religious act at times as the reconnaissance personnel of the Church, exploring new situations as they present themselves. The early days of any new congregation are generally marked by a lack of strict organisation and professionalism as the founding members work together to teach, nurse or care for the unwanted. There is usually little money and local volunteers help. But as the work is established the government moves in demanding professional training and specific standards for buildings and equipment. Grants are given, accounts kept and rules and regulations multiply. Gradually the sisters or brothers are sucked into the system and become for the people they serve part of the power structure.

It takes time before the next generation of incoming religious realise what has happened to their community. This is the moment when sentiment has to be put aside and practical assessments made. It takes faith-filled courage to bring about change, to hand over institutions and to meet the new needs emerging. The alternative is to allow the congregation to die. The life-span of most congregations is around two hundred years.

In the twentieth century it was Pope John XXIII through the Vatican Council who in his prophetic role challenged the religious to renew. During the twelve years allotted to experimentation some congregations decided not to receive new members until they had clarified their ministries and devised more suitable structures. This meant that as the sisters aged there were fewer young members to carry on the work. As institutions were handed over to appropriate authorities most of the sisters undertook individual rather than corporate ministries. In the West this development is suspected of having played into the individualism of the prevailing culture.

Judged from the outside, the sisters seemed to be turning their backs on traditional spiritual values to enjoy those of the secular world. The original withdrawal into the convent, the silence, the time-table that provided daily space for prayer, meals, work, recreation, study and sleep ensured that the sisters were left undisturbed as they lived their routine lifestyle. Now they were available at all times, encouraged to get involved with justice issues and to become aware of the marginalised in their midst. The steady rhythm of community life ceased as the sisters fitted in with the time schedules of seculars. New words like 'burnout' and 'breakdown' were heard until the sisters learned to manage or space their lives more effectively, to delegate, to empower others, to realise that they were not the only ones called to 'labour in the vineyard of the Lord'.

For those sisters who had originally believed themselves called to a life of undisturbed formal prayer and a corporate ministry shared as a member of a community, the renewal proved simply a time of painful upheaval. Yet as they studied the Gospels anew they came to realise that their traditional lifestyle was in some aspects contrary to Gospel values and regulated by men who did not trust women. We are told that the intellect can accept change quite quickly but that there is always a time-lag before the emotions can let go of the past and accept the required changes. Many sisters have undergone that experience over the past twenty years. Perhaps it was made harder by the fact that congregations renewed at differing times and within communities sisters were, for the most part, allowed to adapt at their own rate; and this, of course, led to tension and misunderstandings both within and without the communities.

The Prophetic Role

Jesus did not undertake the role of priest or king; instead he chose that of prophet. In Judaism the prophets were known as 'the conscience of the king'. It was their function to challenge the king whenever he failed to live by the law of God. After his death and resurrection Jesus entrusted his mission to the community he had formed. Therefore, it is the role of the Church to offer an alternative vision to the world, a vision of trust, co-operation and oneness based on justice, which are signs of God's will being accepted on earth. In Judea some prophets became royal courtiers and spoke only what the king wanted to hear. Those who remained faithful to God's calling were persecuted and killed, as was Jesus himself.

At times Church authorities anxious to secure protection for the Christian people conformed to the wishes of emperors and kings. In return they were rewarded with secular power and lands. By the Middle Ages the Church was the most powerful and influential institution in Europe. So what happens when the salt loses its flavour? It was at such times that God raised up religious founders to be a counter-sign pointing once more to the Gospel way of life. Over the centuries the disciples of these prophets, instead of transforming the world, gradually conformed to the standards of the world in order to enable their works to continue. Then the Spirit raised up more prophets and so within the Church there is always a healthy tension between the prophetic voice and human weakness. Sometimes it is the Church leadership that provides the challenge, at other times it is the faithful, often through new religious movements and new forms of religious life, and so by various means the prophetic role in the Church remains active.

Every Christian relates to the Church at two levels. First, to Christ and his Gospel, second to the Church leadership and institutions. Faithfulness to Christ sometimes demands that Christians challenge the conduct not only of the community but of those entrusted with authority. Such Christians are regarded by some as insubordinate, by others as courageous and prophetic.

Religious Life in Transition

It has been acknowledged that women religious had little control over their lifestyle and ministries. In fact they were kept in a borderland, regarded by the laity as part of the clerical structure and by the clergy as extra-devout laity. Today, most women religious are managing to bridge that limbo state by working alongside secular and clerical colleagues. Remembering that 'today is tomorrow's past' it is important that women religious make clear for our contemporary world the meaning of their consecrated lives.

Women religious now in leadership roles within their communities are seeking less authoritarian modes of operating. Canon law and Vatican documents still refer to leaders of religious as 'superiors' despite the fact that many religious find the title absurd in any Christian context. Young Catholics find such military titles as 'the superior general' hilarious. In Ireland the Conference of Major Religious Superiors has recently changed its name to the Conference of Religious of Ireland. In pre-Vatican II days the corporate work of the community usually had priority over the needs and talents of the individual. Many sisters suffered as they struggled with their inadequacies in classroom or hospital ward – as did their pupils and patients. Though each congregation is still entrusted with a specific mission by the Church, today the sisters carry out that mission through a variety of ministries according to the giftedness of each. Apostolic religious no longer carry out their ministries 'on long leads'. The mission of the congregation and the ministry of the religious dictates both the community's and the individual's lifestyle. Pluriformity has replaced uniformity.

Each religious is a member of a praying community and so allots time for daily private prayer as well as regular communal prayer. For the apostolic religious it will seldom take the form of the sung office. Some religious sisters like to make their annual retreat in a monastery where they can join in the solemn worship and savour the silence. Perhaps one of the most significant changes for many religious is in the different approaches to prayer. Older religious were expected to 'recharge their batteries' in the presence of the Blessed Sacrament and so by rule long periods in chapel were set aside for prayer. Today's young apostolic religious, while still practising some of the traditional forms of prayer, are trained to be aware of encountering the Spirit at work in every person and situation and so learn to 'recharge' while involved with others. Their spiritual development demands their attentiveness to the God-within and faith in the promise of Jesus that where two or three are gathered in his name, Christ is present. It requires personal responsibility to become a person of prayer; rules can only regulate the where and how of saying prayers.

Another area of religious life demanding constant evaluation is that of ministry. Some religious dislike the word 'ministry', saying it is only a pious way of talking about one's job. But 'there's the rub'. The dictionary defines work as the application of energy for a purpose, while a job is that energy exerted specifically for payment or profit. Is ministry, that is Christian witness and service, work or a job? Jesus said, 'The labourer is worthy of his hire.' Yet Paul insisted on earning his keep through tent making so that he could minister freely. Most foundresses regarded the necessity to work for one's living as part of the vow of poverty and so the majority of the religious congregations were financially independent, much to the relief of the bishops. The institutions owned by religious not only provided work for their members but offered jobs to seculars as well. Now with religious withdrawing from the ownership and management of institutions, religious not yet eligible for the old-age pension are forced to look for jobs elsewhere and if unsuccessful to apply for State welfare. This is a new experience for religious and brings them more in touch with the reality of many people's lives. Yet it raises questions. Should the income of religious be secured through the carrying out of the mission entrusted to them by the Church? Perhaps it is time the whole Church community participated in the debate. Other topics under discussion at present are: (a) the possibility of temporary religious as is the custom in the Buddhist monasteries; (b) the setting up of mixed communities consisting of married couples, singles and religious. Since Vatican II there has been a rapid increase in the number of lay communities forming around the world.

Some Catholic Views on the Role of Religious

While participating in several meetings lately I heard the views of over two hundred Catholics, women and men, as they discussed the role of religious sisters in the Church of the future. Two women believed that only the contemplative orders should remain, as the ministries of the religious sisters were now the responsibility of the whole community of the Church. The remainder welcomed the sisters moving out of their institutions to live among them as neighbours and co-workers.

Several groups strongly advised religious and clergy to acknowledge that there are subjects about which they know little, e.g. marriage and parenting, and that they should trust Christians with the relevant commitment and experience to minister in these areas. It was also stressed that as religious claimed to be freed by their vow of celibacy to serve wherever needed, it was therefore their role to take risks on behalf of the Church by serving in areas of danger. They specified such ministries as caring for those with contagious diseases, seeking justice for the marginalised in face of government opposition, helping the victims of war in refugee camps, and by travelling abroad to share their spirituality and skills when invited by people in need around the world.

The majority expressed a desire to see religious function in spiritual ministries by providing adult religious education, spiritual direction and counselling, and by empowering others to participate more fully in the mission of Christ. There was also a felt need for religious to be involved in hospice care and in enabling people to accept and appreciate the fact that death is part of our life cycle and experience.

The Future of Apostolic Congregations

First it must be noted that there are in the world today more religious than ever before. They are mostly to be found in the majority world, that is in Asia, Africa and Latin America. In the West their numbers have fallen dramatically. God is indeed calling the young today and the young *are* responding, but religious life no longer provides the main channel through which they live out their response. A growing number of young women and men are qualifying in theology, Scripture, and liturgy. They have part-time jobs, live simply, and married or single they as Church give time to the service of the marginalised at home and abroad. Back in the 1960s these young Catholics would probably have entered the active religious congregations. They too are a 'sign of the times' through which the Spirit speaks.

Those who do respond by joining a religious community are now seldom accepted straight from school. They are expected to have experienced the responsibility of managing their own money, to have learned the necessity for personal integrity when obeying those in authority, and to have realised that it is possible to have loving relationships without becoming sexually involved. New candidates need to have a healthy self-acceptance and learn to sustain the interdependence of community living without being afraid of aloneness. As public persons serving as Church in the world they will have to become aware of justice issues, be prepared to take risks, and be able to live with uncertainty. Above all they will require a strong faith, expressed with hope and joy, and be capable of helping others to trust in God's empowering presence among us.

A newly professed sister told me that during her noviciate she was sent out to experience life in a community of professed sisters. She returned to tell her directress that she was 'setting her up for failure'. She had found little relevance between her training and the form of community life led by the older women. These gaps in a common understanding of the renewal are even greater in the wider Catholic community, and for this reason the noviciate formation often takes place in apprenticeship style with the novice living in a small community as part of the local parish.

This new breed of young religious can be a cause of growth-producing tension in any older community. At one community assembly an older man complained about the self-confidence of, and initiatives taken by the new members. When he sat down one of the new members asked: 'Father, has it not yet occurred to you that we are God's answer to your prayers for vocations?'

The religious life is undergoing another transition in the life of the Christian community and it is hoped that it will be able to break the present log-jam in the Church. It is being Spirit-urged to leave the securities of its institutions and to prepare to meet the new needs of the twenty-first century. Addressing a gathering of religious superiors in Rome in 1990 Cardinal Lorscheider of Brazil said: 'You have the gift of being the first, the pioneers, the spearheads. This is your joy and your specific responsibility.'

PAUSE FOR REFLECTION

1. With which sisters do you empathise most?
   (a) Those delighted with the changes introduced by Vatican II?
   (b) Those grieving over the past while struggling to live the new vision?
   (c) Those resisting change saying: 'The old ways were best'? Why?
2. Describe what you consider the most suitable role for religious sisters today.

6

Women in Ministry

The Gospel Record

According to the Gospels it was to women that the mysteries of Christ's incarnation and resurrection were first revealed. A closer reading of the text shows that women, though seldom mentioned, were among the constant companions of Jesus throughout his public ministry. Jesus travelled from town to town proclaiming the Good News of God's reign. The twelve went with him, as well as some women he had freed of evil spirits and other diseases: Mary of Magdala out of whom he cast seven devils; Joanna the wife of Chusa, a steward in Herod's court; Susanna and 'many other women' who out of their own means supported Jesus and the disciples (Lk. 8:2–3). Scripture scholars tell us that the phrase 'to follow' in the Gospel context refers to discipleship. Mary the mother of Mark, Salome, Mary the wife of Zebedee, Mary the mother of James and Joseph, and Mary the wife of Clopas had 'followed' Jesus while he was in Galilee and had continued with him all the way to Calvary. Mark adds, that 'many other women' had also come to Jerusalem with him (Mk 15:41). These women sacrificed their domestic comforts in order to support Jesus in his ministry.

It is important at this stage to note that all four Evangelists record the feeding of the five thousand men, and two tell of the feeding of four thousand men. Yet only Matthew adds, 'not counting the women and children' (Mt. 14:21 and 15:38 GNB). Here is proof that women, even when involved, were omitted from the sacred records. This leads Christian feminists to ask is it not probable that women were included in the seventy-two? We know they did not figure among the twelve whose number had a specific Jewish significance as representative of the twelve tribes of Israel. Such a significance apparently does not apply to the seventy-two.

Again Jesus chose seventy-two others and sent them out two by two into every town he planned to visit (Lk. 10:1). Unfortunately Matthew did not mention the seventy-two!

The Gospels describe Jesus relating to women with a great openness of mind. He broke taboos in order to engage the Samaritan woman in theological discussion. His choice was sound for she convinced a whole village to come and listen to his teachings (Jn 4). Matthew tells of an encounter with a Gentile woman. It is the only recorded journey outside of Palestine made by Jesus during his public ministry. Jesus refused to heal the daughter of the Canaanite woman saying he had come solely for the people of Israel. Undaunted she challenged Jesus, reminding him that even the dogs were given the crumbs from their master's table. Recognising the Spirit at work in her, Jesus realised that his ministry was not confined to the Jews, that the Gentiles too had the faith necessary to enable miracles to happen (Mt. 15:21–28).

Nor was Jesus ill-at-ease when faced with a woman's emotions. While he was eating in the house of Simon the Pharisee a prostitute entered and proceeded to massage the feet of Jesus. She wept, kissed his feet and dried them with her hair. Knowing that Simon did not approve of the way he was responding, Jesus used the opportunity to speak of compassion: '. . . her many sins have been forgiven – for she loved much' (Lk. 7:36–50 NIV).

Jesus constantly preached that the reign of God would spread only through personal conversion. His was a charismatic renewal, a peace movement in which his followers would act as a leaven in Judaism and the wider society. He had already told the Samaritan woman that the time had come to worship God in Spirit and truth, not in sacred places (Jn 4:23–24). The people of God were to be known by their attitudes, their deeds, their lifestyle in a community of equals where no one lorded it over another (Mt. 20:25–27).

It was a woman, Mary of Magdala, who was the first person commissioned by the Risen Christ to proclaim the Good News (Jn 20:17). Luke records that when Cleopas and his companion returned to Jerusalem with the news that they had seen the Lord 'they found the eleven gathered together *with the others.* Jesus appeared to *them* and said, "You are my witnesses".' Presumably the *you* included those present with the eleven. He then told them to wait in the city until God's power had come down upon them (Lk. 24:13–53 GNB). In the Acts of the Apostles, also written by Luke, it is clearly stated that the eleven gathered in Jerusalem with Mary the mother of Jesus, and the rest of the women and brethren

(Acts 1:14). Therefore feminist scholars consider it reasonable to presume that the Lucan terms 'the others' and 'them' include the women disciples and that they too were in the upper room when the Risen Christ appeared and commissioned all those present to be witnesses to the Good News.

It is sometimes argued that though women were the first to encounter the Risen Christ, according to Jewish custom their witness could not be accepted as official and therefore the men to whom they brought the Good News were the official witnesses of Christianity. Feminists see in Christ's choice of women as his first witnesses a further example of Jesus challenging his disciples to let go of traditional prejudice and together to witness to him as a community of equals.

Women in the Primitive Church

After the Ascension the disciples, women and men, remained in Jerusalem. There they met frequently to pray and Mary, the mother of Jesus, was with them. On one occasion up to 120 believers had gathered together (Acts 1:14–15). Some days later when the promise of the Risen Christ was fulfilled and the power of the Spirit had come upon them Peter went out to an assembled crowd and preached to them quoting the prophet Joel: '. . . I will pour my Spirit on all. Your sons and "daughters" shall prophesy. . . . Even my servants, both men and "women" will receive the Spirit poured out upon them and they shall proclaim my message' (Acts 2:17–18). So in the very first declaration made by a leader of the new Christian community it was acknowledged that the gifts of the Spirit were entrusted to women and men alike.

Persecution became part of the lives of these first Christians. Both women and men were taken from their homes and cast into jail (Acts 8:3). Saul (later Paul) obtained a licence from the high priest to continue the persecution of the Christians who had fled from Jerusalem. While on his journey to Damascus, the Risen Christ challenged Saul and had no hesitation in identifying himself with the men and *women* disciples who were persecuted: 'Saul, Saul! Why do you persecute me?' (Acts 9:4).

The home of Mary, the mother of John whose other name was Mark, became a Church centre. On one occasion when Peter escaped from prison he made his way there and found a large gathering of believers at prayer (Acts 12:12).

Another woman who risked opening her home to a Christian gathering was Lydia, a trader in purple cloth. When Paul and Silas arrived in Philippi they waited until the Sabbath in order to bring the Good News first to the Jews. When they went to the meeting place by the river they found only the women present. To their credit Paul and Silas sat down and spoke to the women about Jesus the Christ. Lydia was baptised with all her household and made her home available to the missionaries. Later when Paul and Silas were released from prison they went straight to Lydia's house and encouraged the believers gathered there. This is the first record of a Christian community in Europe (Acts 16:11–40).

The woman most prominent in the ministry of Paul was Prisca, sometimes referred to by the diminutive Priscilla. She lived in Rome with her husband Aquila. In AD49 the Emperor Claudius ordered all Jews to leave Rome. Prisca and her husband moved to Corinth, where Paul stayed with them and as all three were tent-makers they practised their trade together. Eighteen months later Paul left to return to Palestine. Prisca and Aquila travelled with him as far as Ephesus where they again set up a house-church. While they were in Ephesus a gifted Jewish preacher arrived from Alexandria. He knew only of the baptism of John, so on hearing him preach in the synagogue Prisca and Aquila invited him back to their house and instructed him in the Christian way (Acts 18). By AD58 the couple had returned to Rome, for in his letter to the Romans written in that year Paul greeted Priscilla and Aquila referring to them as co-workers who had risked their lives for him. He added that all the Churches of the Gentiles were grateful to them (Rom. 16:3–5).

There are two other women who, though only mentioned in passing by Paul, have become the subjects of intense debate among scholars today. The first is Phoebe who actually carried Paul's letter to the Roman community and so would have met Prisca. Paul wrote, 'I recommend to you our sister Phoebe who has been a devoted *diakonos* in the church at Cenchrcae. Make her welcome as God's people should and help her when needed. She has been a great help to many, including myself' (Rom. 16:1–2). The use of the word *diakonos* in reference to Phoebe has given rise to debate. Apparently it has no feminine form and this is the first time it is used of a woman. When used of a man it is translated as 'deacon' or 'minister'. Translators in referring to Phoebe often substitute the terms 'helper' or 'servant'. In the Revised Standard Version (1965) and the Jerusalem Bible (1968) the word is translated as 'deaconess'. In the New Revised Standard Version (1991) it is translated as 'deacon'. Some Greek scholars maintain that the most appropriate translation is 'minister', as the word *diakonos* had long been applied to both men and women ministers in the Greek cultic religions.

The debate becomes even more intense when Junia is mentioned (Rom. 16:7). The translations vary. Greetings 'to those outstanding Apostles Andronicus and Junias, my compatriots and fellow prisoners who became Christians before me' (JB). 'Greet Andronicus and Junias, my relatives, who have been in prison with me. They are outstanding among the Apostles, and they were in Christ before I was' (NIV).

The early commentators wrote 'Junia' or 'Julia' and it was surmised that she was part of another ministering couple. However, the term 'apostle' attached to Junia was a problem for some and in later translations the name was altered to Junias. Researchers looking through contemporary documents say that Junia appears but never the masculine form Junias. Today some scholars apply the term 'apostle' to the two but retain the masculine name Junias. Jerome and Chrysostom took for granted that Junia was a woman apostle.

Next we meet two women, Euodia and Syntyche, of whom Paul writes, '. . . these women have laboured side by side with me in the Gospel together with Clement and the rest of my co-workers. They ministered in the Church at Philippi founded by Lydia.' Paul is concerned because there is some quarrel between them. He pleads with them to come to an agreement and asks Syzygus to help achieve a reconciliation (Phil. 4:2–3). Paul understood such quarrels, considering the serious differences he had had with Barnabas (Acts 15:36–40) and Peter (Gal. 2:11–14). Commentators conclude that Euodia and Syntyche must have been church leaders, hence Paul's urgent concern.

Paul founded charismatic Churches which accepted that the gifts of the Holy Spirit were bestowed on the members irrespective of class, race or sex. Therefore it is not surprising to find women ministers leading house-churches, teaching and travelling abroad on mission. Despite this we know that the records fail to do justice to the role women played in the Christ story. For example Paul wrote: 'Christ appeared first to Cephas, then to the twelve. Next he revealed himself to five hundred of the brethren at once, some are still alive, but some are dead; after that he appeared to James and then to all the apostles. Last of all he appeared to me, as one born out of time' (1 Cor. 15:5–8). Not a word about the appearances to the women at the tomb!

Paul's letters were written between AD51–63. The pseudo-Pauline letters were written after Paul's death from around AD65 to well into the second century. They were written by second- and third-generation members of the Churches founded by Paul and take a more organisational approach to church life. They are the letters to the Ephesians, Colossians, Titus and Timothy. Scholars also believe that some of Paul's own letters have had passages inserted at a later date as their tone does not harmonise with the charismatic leadership given by Paul. Passages exhorting women to be submissive to their husbands (Eph. 5:22 and Col. 3:18) or directing them not to teach but to be saved through child-bearing (1 Tim. 2:12–15) could hardly have been meant for Priscilla. Similarly the passage which tells women not to speak at religious meetings but to question their husbands at home (1 Cor. 14:34–35) would have puzzled Phoebe who was actually a *diakonos* in one of the Corinthian churches. Nor could it have been intended for the many Christian women married to non-believers. Such directions clearly come from a later generation. Being under constant persecution it was understandable that compromises were made but we have to be careful not to accept these compromises as part of the Good News.

It is clear that in the early Church ministry was allocated according to the individual's gifts and was associated with teaching and community building rather than with the Eucharist. In the Didache, a document of the Church in Antioch written at the end of the first century, we learn that prophets and teachers were entrusted with the leadership of the community. On the day of Pentecost Peter proclaimed to the people the words of the prophet Joel, 'your daughters will prophesy' and we find this promise fulfilled in the four daughters of Philip who exercised their ministry in Caesarea (Acts 21:9). From their study of the Scripture accounts feminists conclude that women and men shared equally in the ministry of the early Church.

The First Millennium

Documents referring to women in ministry are few, so feminist researchers have had to supplement the written records with tomb inscriptions. These latter are found mostly in the Eastern Church where women continued in ordained ministry up until the twelfth century, whereas in the Roman Church they disappeared from the records after the sixth century. There were eventually three canonical orders for women: they were ordained as deacons, appointed into the order of widows, or became consecrated virgins.

In AD112 two women deacons were tortured in Bithynia. From the letters of the governor Pliny the Younger to the Emperor Trajan we learn that both women and slaves were ordained into Christian ministry. The two women suffered in Bithynia because of the success of their ministry. As the number of Christian converts increased, the sale of animals for sacrifice decreased, so the butchers of the province protested.

About AD170 the prophetesses Maximilla and Prisca, co-ministers with Montanus, caused great division in the Church. Their followers objected to the bishops assuming more and more authority while down-grading the leadership of prophets. The three were denounced as heretics. It is believed that this move against Prisca and Maximilla marks the beginning of official antagonism towards women in Church leadership. From now on it is notable that groups declared heretical by the Fathers had all accepted the leadership of women.

The *Didascalis Apostolorum* (Teachings of the Apostles) was written in Syria in the third century. By now the bishop had become the centre of unity in the local Church and was acknowledged as the teacher of orthodoxy. It states that women are no longer to teach, 'concerning Christ and his redemptive Passion. For you, oh women, were not appointed to teach. The Lord Jesus Christ, our Master, sent the Twelve to teach the people and the Gentiles, and there were no women amongst us.' Yet the Council of Chalcedon (451) speaks of the ordination of women deacons.[1]

Olympias, Pentadia and Amprucla were ordained deacons serving in the Church of Sa Sophia in Constantinople. It seems that the ministry of the women deacons was confined to the service of the women in the community. They instructed women for baptism, led them to the font, anointed their bodies and continued to accompany the newly baptised in their practice of the faith. They ministered to the dying and to those in prison, and cared for the sick and orphans. Romana, a fourth-century deaconess in the Church at Antioch was appointed by the bishop to care for prostitutes.

In Rome the young widow Marcella gathered a group of women together, among them Fabiola, Lea, Felicitas and Asella. They lived in their own homes but followed a rule and met for study and prayer. Marcella learned Greek and Aramaic and when Jerome arrived in Rome as secretary to Pope Damasus he discussed the Scriptures with the group. Marcella was so eager to learn that Jerome accused her of slave-driving him.

By the end of the fourth century Cyril, Bishop of Jerusalem, wrote forbidding women to administer baptism and directing them not to let their voices be heard at public prayer. There seems to have been no universal teaching on the ministry of women as yet. Rules and regulations applied locally. Most of the women deacons were ordained in the Eastern Church; however there is a fifth-century reference to the deacon Hilaria, daughter of Remy, Bishop of Rheims. Yet it was in France that the *Statuta Ecclesiae Antiqua* originated at this time. In them Canon 37 states that a woman, no matter how learned and holy, was not to teach men in assembly. Gone was the recognition that the Spirit's gifts were bestowed on women and men alike.

Over in Germany the *Visigothic Sacramentary*, also produced in the fifth century, had the same rite for installing abbots and abbesses, the pallium and mitre being given to both. Brigid of Ireland, as Abbess in Kildare, exercised the jurisdiction of a bishop, though it is believed Conleth consecrated at the Eucharists over which she presided.

In 535 the Emperor Justinian laid down that in Constantinople women deacons who were to conduct the ceremony of baptism must be widows or virgins over fifty years of age. However by 829 complaints were made at the Reforming Synod of Paris about women touching the holy vessels, dispensing the sacred host and standing near the altar.

The Second Millennium

Just as the right of the Empress Eudoxia to participate in Church affairs had been accepted in Constantinople, so now in the eleventh century we find dissenting clerics accepting regulations laid down by Margaret, Queen of Scotland, at their local synod. One of the problems concerned the reception of the sacred host. Some of the clergy feared Paul's warning against sacrilege. Margaret argued that Paul was speaking of those who treated the sacred host as ordinary food, that in fact all of us are sinners but to refuse to receive was to contradict the words of Jesus: 'unless you eat my body and drink my blood you cannot have life in you' (Jn 6:53). It is believed that the religious authority of royal women was received at their consecration as Queen.

Another group of women invested with religious authority were the abbesses. They also attended synods, held jurisdiction beyond the monastery and gave sacramental absolution to the members of their communities. Hildegard of Bingen, a Benedictine Abbess in the twelfth century, preached publicly, and to the bishops and clergy assembled in synod.

During the twelfth century the theology of priesthood and sacrament was separated from the theology of Church as community. This development affected the ministry of women who no longer performed altar duties because of 'the defilement of menstruation'. They were now confined to directing monastic communities of women. Even the canonesses who had served in the cathedrals and ministered there to women were now ordered to follow a monastic lifestyle complete with enclosure. They protested saying that it was not their calling in the Church.

During the thirteenth and fourteenth centuries there spread from the Netherlands groupings of women known as the Beguines. They did not take vows and retained control over their own money which was often earned through their cloth industries. Outside working hours they served poor women, taught children and cared for the sick. Contemporary society was challenged by their simple lifestyle. The Beguines functioned outside the control system of the clergy and the records tell of various ruses undertaken by bishops in their efforts to impose enclosure, until finally the Beguine movement was forced to disband.

Throughout Church history, groups in which women played a leadership role were frequently declared heretical. Heretics were not only those who challenged Church teaching, but also those who disregarded Church discipline. Feminists ask: Were Church authorities so prejudiced that any movement led by women was to be condemned? Or did the Church so marginalise women that they moved into groups in which they knew their God-given talents would be employed?

Canon 813 of the 1917 Code on the question of altar servers stated: 'A female person may not minister. An exception is allowed only if no male person can be had and there is a good reason. But female persons may in no case come up to the altar, and may only give responses from afar.' The post-Vatican II document *Musicam Sacram of 1976* on music in the liturgy rules that, '. . . Where there are women members, the choir's place is to be outside the sanctuary' (n. 23). Though official, this regulation is constantly ignored and from March 2007 it will become redundant – Canon 26 of the 1983 Code says: '. . . a custom which is contrary to the canon law currently in force, or is apart from the canon law, acquires the force of law only when it has been lawfully observed for a period of thirty continuous and complete years.' Canon 27 says: 'Custom is the best interpreter of Law.'

Considered ritually unclean, women by the end of the nineteenth century were not only forbidden in the sanctuary but to actually sing in choirs. In order to provide the high treble voices for religious ceremonies the Greek Church allowed the castration of boy sopranos. In 1748 Pope Benedict XIV introduced *castrati* into Rome. There they were feted as stars. Alphonsus Liguori, theologian and founder of the Redemptorists, questioned the morality of castrating boys so that as men they might sing the praises of God with the voices of women. The last of the castrati to sing in St Peter's died in 1924.

Women in Ministry Today

Many clergy are still trained into a system of control. Women, therefore, have been obliged to live their faith within a patriarchal Church, pray in a male-oriented language, confess sins as defined by men, and receive sacramental grace in accordance with the decisions of men. Women dream of the day when in the Church they can live their lives as women. Throughout the world there are devout women who feel alienated and angry. Some have gone beyond anger into apathy. Others are willing to educate themselves to work constructively for the future and to build on the pioneer work of the women who have gone before. Their aim is not the clericalisation of women but the declericalisation of the Church. They believe Jesus left us guidelines for a community on mission, not directives for a patriarchal organisation.

Christian feminists seek a Church leadership that is answerable to the community. When the hierarchy, without consultation, pronounces on issues specific to women, feminists see it as their duty to object, to refuse to be ignored, treated as minors, and denied adult Christian responsibilities. They ask that clerical attitudes be in keeping with the dignity of women. When treated as the source of man's temptations, woman is marginalised. When romanticised and placed on a pedestal she is removed from the centre of Church affairs. In the United States of America 25 per cent of religious sisters hold doctorates while only 10 per cent of bishops are equally qualified. Yet women are forbidden to preach simply because of their sex – one priest suggested they write books of homilies for their less qualified brethren.[2]

Ministry is a Christian obligation, we are a Church of the baptised not of the ordained. This primacy of baptism is important when considering the role of women in the Church. Both men and women ask why is it that after baptism a woman's sex becomes an obstacle to her full participation in Christian ministry? Christian feminists are as yet divided on how best to proceed. Some advocate 'A Phoebe Push' seeking to have women ordained into the permanent diaconate. Others react in horror saying the permanent diaconate simply adds a lower rung to the hierarchical ladder and ordains men for ministries already carried out by women.

Ministry is described as the use of one's talents in union with Christ for the good of others. Women ministers are those women who carry out their work as Church. They hand on the faith in their homes, bring healing to the broken, teach, and are active in many charitable projects. Today women engage in ministries that were once the preserve of clerics. They work in Vatican offices, they are diocesan administrators, chancellors, canon lawyers, school supervisors, lecturers in seminaries, members of marriage tribunals, secretaries to bishops' conferences, chaplains in hospitals, colleges and prisons. In parishes they carry out pastoral work and conduct Communion services. They are also engaged in spiritual counselling, and in academic research. It is suggested that women could make effective papal nuncios.

Sometimes the question is raised as to what new dimension women can bring to ministry. There is a danger here of accepting the male stereotyping of the feminine and so answering that women would be more caring, compassionate, dedicated and persevering, etc., which of course is not true. What is true though is that women have a different experience of embodiment and have a different perspective on incarnation. They know what it is to be marginalised and excluded in the Church and therefore can relate to those at the margins of society. They have an underview of authority at work. It has been said that women see 'circles not ladders', which is essential for an understanding of the trinitarian community we call God.

All feminists are agreed on encouraging women to study theology, Scripture, sociology, Church history and other disciplines; and to acquire skills in leadership, communication and peace-making; to network with women in other churches and religions, and to dialogue with men. Catholic feminists do not claim that women in leadership or ordained ministry will make the

Church more holy, more compassionate, what they do claim is that by ordaining women the organisation of the Church will become more just and more in conformity with the Gospel message.

PAUSE FOR REFLECTION

1. Which Church ministries have helped you most in your spiritual, community and domestic life?
2. Is the Good News Jesus brought to women bad news for men? Why?

7

The Ordination of Women

During the past three decades the Roman Catholic Church has undertaken intensive studies on the question of women's participation in ministry. Over the years there have been biblical, theological, canonical, historical and sociological studies on the subject. In the 1976 document *Inter Insigniores* the Congregation for the Doctrine of the Faith stated that '. . . the Church in fidelity to the example of the Lord, does not consider herself authorised to admit women to priestly ordination.' This phraseology upset many Catholics. They asked: We were not consulted so how can the authorities know what the Church thinks? However, Hermann Josef Pottmeyer, a member of the International Theological Commission, agrees that for the pope on his own authority to go against tradition would be sheer papalism. He says, 'The proper forum for a decision in a matter of this kind is a Council.'[1] The official reasons against the ordination of women can be dealt with under three headings: Scripture, tradition and christology.

Scripture

Those who argue against the ordination of women say that it is clear from Scripture that Jesus founded the Christian priesthood on the twelve. Later when the twelve were reduced to eleven, it was a man, Matthias, who was chosen to replace Judas (Acts 1:26). It is pointed out that Jesus broke many taboos in favour of women therefore their exclusion from the twelve would seem to indicate a deliberate decision on the part of Jesus. It was to the twelve that Jesus gave the power to consecrate the eucharistic bread (Lk. 22:19).

When the Church spread into the Greco-Roman world, where women priests were the norm in the cultic religions, the Christian community still refrained from ordaining women. It is pointed out that the twelve were prepared to act contrary to the Mosaic law by receiving uncircumcised Gentiles into the community and even into the priesthood. So it is argued that the exclusion of women was understood to be in accordance with the mind of Jesus.

Refuting these arguments are those who believe that today the ordination of women is essential for the credibility of the Church in fulfilling its mission to the world. They agree that there was no woman among the twelve, but add that the twelve is a rather vague group on which to rest any arguments. The function of the twelve, they say, was to show a symbolic continuity with the twelve tribes of Israel, and the twelve should not be confused with apostleship or apostleship with priesthood (as explained in Chapter 4 of this book).

As regards the Last Supper, if it was the Passover meal, then they argue that the women and children were present. Some commentators, in trying to overcome certain difficulties concerning dates, suggest that it was not the Passover meal. That would justify the absence of women as it was the Jewish custom for women and men to eat apart except during ritual meals. However, Luke states specifically that it was the Passover meal (Lk. 22:7–21). Others ask whether the women who were to follow Jesus to Calvary could be excluded from this sacred ritual meal of the Jews?

The fact that the women are not mentioned as being among those present is no surprise, as three of the Evangelists failed to record their presence among the five thousand who were fed with the loaves and fishes. From the study of the Passion accounts some scholars hold that the power to celebrate the Eucharist was given by Jesus to the entire Christian community and not just to twelve individuals.

Again those who are anxious to see women ordained agree that in the Christian Scriptures there is no evidence of a woman ministering as a priest. Nor, they insist, is there any record of a Christian man acting in a priestly capacity. To argue from what Jesus did not do could go on for ever without leading to any accurate conclusions. For, they say, Jesus did not include Gentiles among the twelve. He did not restrict the twelve to those who were celibate. He did not tell the man caught in adultery to 'sin no more'. He did not denounce slavery, and so on.

In the 1970s the Pontifical Biblical Commission advised Pope Paul VI that they could find no clear indications in the Scriptures of Christ's will on the questions about the ordination of women to the priesthood, and that the decision to exclude women could not be safely based on Scripture alone.

Tradition

If it is accepted that Scripture is not sufficiently clear on the question of Christian priesthood, then the next step is to review the tradition. It is known that during the second century the Gnostics and Montanists appointed women who sometimes presided at the Eucharist. This practice was rejected by Irenaeus, Cyprian and Origen who regarded both groups as heretical. An Egyptian document of AD300, the *Apostolic Church Order*, states: 'When the Master prayed over the bread and the cup, and blessed them saying, "This is my body and blood", he did not allow women to stand with us.'

The First Council of Orange held in 441 declared: 'Deaconesses are absolutely not to be ordained; and if there are still any of them, let them bow their heads under the benediction that is given to the congregation.' Pope Gelasius wrote to the bishops of Italy protesting that women were discharging altar service allowed only to men. The Vincention Code of the same century states that revelation was finalised in Christ and that nothing new may be introduced. Therefore, to ordain women would be to go against tradition.

During the Middle Ages the Waldensians and Cathari appointed women to preside at the Eucharist but by the twelfth century these communities were excommunicated. Both groups continued as independent Churches. Around this time Hildegarde, Abbess of the Bingen monastery, rejected outright the idea of ordaining a woman to priesthood.

The Dominican theologian, Thomas Aquinas, who taught in the thirteenth century, held that a woman could not receive holy orders because the priestly state involved ruling the faithful, whereas a woman by her very nature is subject to man, even though at the personal level she can excel a man in her natural giftedness. His contemporary, Duns Scotus, held that the main reason for excluding women from priesthood was the fact that it was so ordained by Jesus, otherwise the Church would not have presumed to deny the female sex.

Thus the Fathers, the medieval Church and the classical theologians taught that the ordination of women was contrary to the will of Christ as received through tradition. Today those who oppose the ordination of women say that the Church leadership is not anti-woman but is Spirit-led and faithful to the mind of Christ.

Those in favour of the ordination of women argue that the tradition is based on flawed interpretations of Genesis 2:20–22 in which woman is said to be created as a helper to man, and Genesis 3:16 in which God told Eve that part of her punishment was to be subject to her husband. From these passages Augustine came to make such statements as, 'By the natural order women must be subject to men and children to their parents. It is a matter of justice that the weaker reason be subject to the stronger.' Church leaders are accused of continuing to legislate according to these same prejudices. Modern biblical and theological research is questioning the tradition and the assumptions that have been passed on concerning Christian priesthood. It has been pointed out that 'tradition is not a closed and finished book. It is the book so far – we are now writing the next chapter. You must not confuse the word tradition with the word magisterium.'[2] Professor Mary McAleese, of Queen's University Belfast, speaking at a BASIC seminar held in Dublin on 25 March 1995 reminded those present that 'in Northern Ireland tradition causes death'.

'In the Person of Christ'

A further argument against the ordination of women rests on the fact that Jesus was a man. Some hold that the role of the ordained priest is to stand as a man in the place of the man Jesus. Following on from this is the belief that the priest who says 'This is my Body' must be a man. The Church has power over the administration of the sacraments, not over their substance. Just as you cannot substitute other food for bread and wine, so a woman may not replace a man.

Another reason given in support of opposing the ordination of women is the centrality of the spousal image given of the relationship between Christ and the Church (Mt. 9:15; Jn 3:29; 2 Cor. 11:2; Eph. 5:22–23; Rev. 19:7 and 21:9). This spousal sign is claimed to be essential to the sacrament of ordination. As the Church is referred to as the Bride of Christ, the symbolism requires that the priest who acts 'in the person of Christ' be male. Furthermore, the Scriptures explicitly state: 'It is the custom in all the Churches of God's people for the women to remain in silence during meetings. They should not speak as the Jewish law lays down. Women are not to be in charge' (1 Cor. 14:33–34). In the thirteenth century the Franciscan Bonaventure held that the priest represented Christ as head and bridegroom, that in this sacrament the person ordained is a sign of Christ the mediator.

It is argued that the leadership of men and subordination of women was not caused by the prevailing patriarchal societies of the times, but was the deliberate choice of the Christian community modelled on Christ's spousal relationship with the Church. In Colossians 3:18–25 wives, children and slaves are to be subject to the husband, father, master, who in turn must love and treat with justice those in his care. The spousal image is made clearer in Ephesians 5:21–23 where the headship and subordination relationship between husband and wife is said to symbolise the relationship between Christ and his Church. Some hold that the obligation to love demands greater self-sacrifice than the obligation to submit and that to interfere with the hierarchical structure in marriage would weaken the central symbol of Christ's relationship with the Church.

In response the pro-ordination lobby says that to suggest that the priest represents the bridegroom is unsustainable. Christ is not a bridegroom but loves as a bridegroom should. To take the metaphor literally destroys the argument as in the symbolism used Christ is bridegroom to the whole Church, not just to its female members.

Do Christian feminists have a problem with the maleness of Jesus? The answer is no – their problem is with clerical authorities who give the maleness of Jesus priority over the humanity he shared with women and men alike. In the early Church the *alter Christus* was the community of the baptised, not of the ordained.

When in the fourth century Appolinarius declared that Jesus was not fully human and that only the spiritual was redeemed, Gregory of Nasianzus refuted his teaching with the famous phrase, 'What is not assumed is not redeemed.' Jesus in assuming our humanity did not assume femaleness, so are women redeemed? Has the maleness of Christ become part of the 'economy of salvation'? Such are the questions asked. Many see this attitude as bordering on heresy. Is maleness a passport into the sacred place where God is encountered? Is femaleness a spiritual impediment, a sacramental obstacle? Can a woman be a Christ-like person? Why are women baptised into the (male) Body of Christ?

Scholars who study every aspect of the question with a view to promoting the ordination of women claim that there is no evidence whatsoever that these negative attitudes to femaleness represent the mind of Christ. '. . . where two or three meet in my name, I shall be there with them' (Mt. 18:20JB). There is no mention here of the two or three being male, not even the one who presides. On the road to Damascus the Risen Christ appeared to Saul saying: 'I am Jesus, and you are persecuting me' (Acts 9:3–5JB). Saul was about to arrest all those, men and *women*, who he found followed the Way.

Second-century martyrs had no difficulty in recognising Christ in a woman.

> Blandina was hung on a post and exposed as bait for the wild animals that were let loose on her. She seemed to hang there in the form of a cross, and by her fervent prayer she aroused intense enthusiasm in those who were undergoing their ordeal, for in their torment with their physical eyes they saw in the person of their sister him who was crucified for them. . . . Tiny, weak, and insignificant as she was she would give inspiration to her brothers, for she had put on Christ . . .
>
> (*Acts of the Martyrs*)

Vatican observers note that it is only since it was admitted that the tradition is biased against women, that the maleness of Jesus has become the main argument for maintaining the *status quo.* Jesus, it is pointed out, placed little importance on any family relationship with himself, saying that his brothers and sisters were those who did the will of the Father (Mk 3:31–35). The Christian is identified with the ministering Christ through the practice of faith and love, not through any physical resemblance to Jesus. In some Christian Churches it is acceptable for the Risen Christ to be represented by the priest, by the people gathered together, by bread and wine, the image of a lamb or fish, but not by a woman.

In the past the people, female and male, celebrated the Eucharist as 'the body of Christ'. How or when did it come about that the focus was placed on the priest as acting in the person of Christ? The answer apparently lies with Jerome who died in AD420. In 2 Corinthian 2:10 Paul wrote, 'Whenever I have forgiven another, I have done so in the *presence* of Christ for your benefit.' Jerome in translating this passage into Latin wrote: '*in persona Christi*' (in the person of Christ). And so all the vernacular translations of the Bible from Jerome's Latin perpetuated his translation 'in the person of Christ'. Translations in use today have returned to the original wording 'in the presence of Christ'.

The priest acts '*in persona eccleie*' on behalf of the Church. The prayers of the Mass make this clear as the priest constantly addresses Christ, 'Christ, have mercy on us' etc. The *Constitution on the Sacred Liturgy* (1963), states: 'By his power he is present in the sacraments so that when anybody baptises it is really Christ himself who baptises. He is present in his word since it is he himself who speaks when holy scriptures are read in Church' (a.7). Women in the Catholic Church baptise and read the Word aloud at Mass.

Paul wrote: 'In baptism there is neither Jew nor Gentile, slave or free, male or female, for you are all one in Jesus, the Christ' (Gal. 3:28). Yet according to a later Church tradition it was acceptable to call Jews 'perfidious' even in our solemn rituals, and for Christians to buy people as slaves. Church attitudes reflected the great divisions in society that Christ had come to heal. In modern times the Church has officially rejected slavery and racism, especially anti-Semitism. It now remains for the great wound of sexism to be healed so that the Church may be presented more whole to the world.

Unclean

One impediment that is not raised today by theologians opposed to the ordination of women is the age-old belief that women are ritually unclean. The Jewish law laid down that a menstruating woman was unclean for seven days and that anyone she touched or anything she sat on became unclean for certain prescribed periods (Lev. 15:19–30).

At the beginning of the seventh century Gregory the Great (died AD604) ruled that women were not to be refused entrance to church during menstruation or pregnancy. However a 1572 canon law forbade women to receive Holy Communion for several weeks after childbirth. Right into the twentieth century Catholic women were expected to undergo the purification ceremony of churching after childbirth. Some women believe that the blood taboo is still at the core of the opposition to women in the ordained ministry. While the Church leaders extol motherhood, they see potential motherhood as making women unfit for ordination.[3] The physical nature of women has been downgraded for so long that there is a need now for women to affirm their femaleness. Jesus made it clear that purity laws were not the means through which access was gained to the divine life; for that repentance and compassion were the requirements.

A Renewed Priesthood

Today's priesthood is seen as too masculine, too focused on maintenance and control. It has been noticed that when clerics discuss the ordination of women many confine their arguments to tradition and regulations, they do not consider how best to serve the Good News. They do not ask if the present form of priesthood is liberating or inhibiting the community.

The present structures are at variance with the Gospel and make the use of the laity's gifts dependent on the good will of the clergy. More and more women are finding the all-male priesthood difficult to endure and point out that at the altar the priests dress like women, do 'women's work' by washing up, but serve themselves first. Defending the male monopoly, some declare, is like defending the 'divine right of kings'.

The issue is not the rejection of leadership and institutionalised power, but how it is used or abused, and how best it can be structured. The priesthood as it is today was not a practice of the primitive Church, it evolved. The maintenance group in the Church argues that to allow priestly practice to evolve further would suggest that the Church had been wrong over the past two thousand years, and so it is not feasible to consider the ordination of women.

No woman or man has a right to ordination, but the Christian community has a right to acceptable leadership and to the Eucharist. The community also has the right to choose its own ministers on the basis of their God-given gifts, not on the grounds of sex. Women offering themselves for ministry are accused of seeking power, young men are presumed to be consumed with a desire to serve the community. Most Catholic women claim that they do not wish to see women ordained into clericalism, wearing the clerical collar, being called Reverend and receiving status privileges. They envisage a renewed priestly ministry, a more inclusive priesthood, for they believe that it is not just the ordination of women but the recognition of a wider range of ministries that will transform authority structures in the Church.

Some people claim that the ordination of women in the Roman Catholic Church will hinder the process of Church unity. Women reject having the burden of unity placed on them, and point out that the Anglican communion has been ordaining women since 1947 and this has not hindered dialogue taking place officially between Rome and Canterbury over the past three decades.

Jackie Hawkins, speaking at the BASIC seminar already mentioned, told how it was the Protestant women among whom she worked who first made her aware of her call to the ordained ministry. She compared her experience of this call to that of an earlier experience when she gave birth to a stillborn infant. 'My daughter,' she said, 'had no reality for anyone save myself; so it is with this call growing within me.' It was suggested to her that if she wished to be taken seriously by the establishment she should stop wearing ear-rings – and this, she exclaimed, from clerics who bedeck themselves in jewelled pectoral crosses, rings and embroidered garments![4]

An Issue of Credibility

The ordination of women was not high on the Christian feminist agenda until it became obvious that the attitude of Church leaders towards women was undermining the credibility of the Church as it preached the Good News, especially to women.

In his *Letter to Women* published in June 1995, shortly before the UN Fourth World Conference on Women held in Beijing, Pope John Paul II began by thanking women for their contribution to both domestic and public life and for their insights which 'help to make human relations more honest and authentic'. He admitted that obstacles had been placed in the way of women's progress and that they had been marginalised. Where church members had contributed to this situation he declared, 'for this, I am truly sorry' (n. 3). He continued: 'there is an urgent need to achieve *real equality* in every area' (n. 4). He supported equal pay for equal work, condemned violence against women, foretold that women would play a leading role in solving world problems and admired the courage of those who had struggled for the rights of women. He reinterpreted Genesis 1 and 2 in favour of women.

As women read the Letter many checked to see if the signature was truly that of John Paul II – it was. Women journalists expressed disbelief, amazement and then relief that in their struggle for justice they now had the support of the leader of the Catholic Church. The Pope called for a '*campaign for the promotion of women*, concentrating on all areas of women's life . . .' (n. 6). They read on with renewed hope until they came to the section where they are told that Christ 'entrusted only to men the task of being *an "icon" of his countenance as "shepherd" and "bridegroom" of the Church through the exercise of the ministerial priesthood . . .*' (n. 11). The italics are the Pope's own and at this point his Letter was dropped into many a waste-paper basket.

The ordination of women is not a 'women's issue' but a Church issue affecting the credibility of the Church in its moral teachings and its opposition to injustice. By denying ordination to women, women are denied access to decision-making, where what John Paul II called the 'genius of women' (n. 10) could be used effectively for the good of the Church and the world. At present, canonists are considering practical ways of reintroducing the earlier Church practice when jurisdiction and ordination were totally separated. Christian feminists hold that to ordain women would have the symbolic importance of witnessing to the world that women are equally created in the image of God and that the Roman Catholic Church has overcome the sin of sexism. They believe the problem is not to do with flesh and blood only, but with history and tradition. Today the question of the ordination of women is seen to be as radical and as important to the future of the Church as was the decision made by the first Jewish Christians to accept Gentile men into the community without subjecting them to circumcision (Acts 15). One priest, Pádraig Standún, aware of this, stated in a homily given at Maynooth in June 1996, that unless the Church ordained women it would die as an institution. 'Right now the Spirit is saying above all else to the Churches: "Women are equal, women are equal, women are equal."'[5]

A renewed priesthood requires not only the inclusion of women but the restructuring of the hierarchical system and the commissioning of a wider range of ministries. The campaign for the ordination of women is said to be the outcome of the present inadequate model of priesthood, the bitter fruit of clericalism. If women were admitted into the present structure there would be the danger of men expecting women to conform to their model of service and thus women would fail to bring about change.

In 1962 a Swiss woman sent the first formal application received by Rome from a woman seeking ordination. Thirty years later in 1992 Soline Vatinal, a French woman married to an Irish man, asked to be ordained. The couple together with a priest founded BASIC, Brothers and Sisters in Christ, an Irish-based network of women and men. At the end of Soline's address given at the BASIC seminar in 1995, a member of an association of married priests, now denied priestly ministry, stood up and said, 'We understand your pain.'

In 1994, when Rome produced a document entitled *On Reserving Priestly Ordination to Men Alone* Soline responded: 'God said, "It is not good that the man should be alone"' (Gen. 2:18 JB).

PAUSE FOR REFLECTION

1. When Jesus as Christ is presented as African or Asian, transcending race, it is accepted. When presented as a woman, transcending sex, it causes upset. Why ?
2. How do you see the credibility of the Church affected by the ordination or the non-ordination of women ?

8

Womanists

The brief survey of attitudes towards women in the Church, given in the previous chapters, shows how over the past fifty years the awareness raised by feminists has enabled many men and women to realise just how negative those attitudes had become. This awareness inspired Pope John Paul II to apologise to women on behalf of the Church. In *An Introduction to Christian Feminism*[1] I have explained how it took me six years to discover that feminists do not speak with one voice. The various strands of feminism have their beginnings in different historical circumstances, times and places, and in my earlier book I described some of the areas in which feminists' views differ and some in which they agree. Since then I have been brought into contact with the thinking of women not of the white race, some of whom refer to their perspective as 'womanism'.

Womanism – Feminism

Feminism comes from the experience of white middle-class Western women and focuses on the sexism prevalent in a patriarchal society. However, patriarchal oppression is experienced differently by women. While white married middle-class American women rebelled at the social convention which confined them to the home, the African-American woman dreamed of giving up work to tend her family full time. Womanism, while also focused on sexism, includes racism and classism as well. It is said that feminism is to womanism what mauve is to purple.

Womanists regard feminism as a luxury as far as their own experience is concerned. White feminists seem at times to be oblivious to the sufferings endured by other women through racism and classism. The racist oppression of coloured people is far greater than any oppression of men over women. Many white feminists overlook the fact that they have themselves oppressed both coloured and working-class women, e.g. the low pay offered to their child minders and domestic helps. It is time for women to make a study of women as oppressors, and to study how they are perceived by each other.

Women are divided by race, class, culture, religion, age, education, lifestyle, status and language. Therefore, it behoves feminists to be wary when making cross-cultural judgments. For example, feminists rightly condemn female genital mutilation but fail to compare it with the bodily mutilations Western women undergo – such as breast enlargements – in order to make themselves more pleasing to men. Nor are feminists always sensitive to the facts of history. It is pointed out that for some Americans the annual Thanksgiving Day celebration is a day of mourning. When the founding fathers of the United States claimed that all men had an inalienable right to own property, they were referring to white men. Black men were counted as property. This double perspective became apparent in Latin America when in 1992 attempts were made to celebrate the fifth centenary of the 'discovery' of America.

If white feminists are to become credible they, like patriarchal men, need to first repent of their treatment and neglect of coloured women. This is especially true of women colonists, who, like their men, regarded themselves as superior to the women and men they helped to colonise. So complete was the damage done to a subject people that black women had to learn that 'black is beautiful'. In a talk given at Maynooth in November 1994, Teresa Okure SHCJ pointed out that missionaries who, unlike Jesus, did not become one with the people, acted as colonisers by belittling the cultural values of the Africans and thus causing them to despise themselves.[2]

Christianity and Inculturation

After the death and resurrection of Jesus the first Christians brought the faith beyond the synagogues and out into other cultures. This meant they had to consider the relevance of the Jewish law for other peoples. This problem was solved for them when during their travels they recognised the Spirit of God present within diverse cultures, and Paul could write that in Christ Jesus there was no longer any distinction of race, class or sex (Gal. 3:28). Eventually the momentous decision was made that circumcision was no longer necessary and that kosher rules did not apply to Gentile Christians. In Athens Paul had to learn how best to present the faith within the culture there (Acts 17:16–34). Later Patrick had to do the same in Ireland, hence the famous Celtic cross in which the circle of the sun supports the outstretched arms of the cross.

Church cultural adaptation seems to have ceased when the centre of Church power became permanently established in Rome. With few exceptions, to Christianise meant to Westernise. Christianity had been literally so clothed in Western robes – clerical and religious dress – that an extra cultural layer was imposed on non-Europeans when they came 'to put on Christ'. In fact the missionaries are accused of having tried to put trousers on Jesus. The Christianity brought to central and southern Africa was already flawed, riddled with divisions caused by the political wars in Europe. Villages that had been united were divided as rival Christian Churches showed contempt for each other. One Nigerian Bishop said to me, 'We want Christ and the Gospel, not your European history and prejudices.' Missionaries in Ghana brought confusion to the Ewe women who enjoyed a higher status within their society than that allowed them in the Church, yet the missionaries claimed they were bringing Good News!

Womanist Theology

The Circle of Concerned African Women Theologians are engaged in the quest for a better understanding of the Scriptures as they relate to women. Approaching the Bible as a community book to be interpreted by the community, they work in common with the Ecumenical Association of Third World Theologians, with men and with non-scholars. These women work not only from their experience of being female but also from their experience of being black – hence the importance they attach to including their non-white brothers in the research. They believe that a coloured man's experience of racism will enable him to see more clearly the injustices inherent in sexism.

The African women theologians maintain that modern Western civilisation with its characteristic individualism has subverted the Gospel message. Teresa Okure points out that Mary of Magdala was the first person the Risen Christ commissioned to proclaim the Good News. And what was this Good News? Not to tell that Jesus was risen; that was the information given by the angels. The message Jesus gave was: 'tell them, "I am returning to my Father and your Father, to my God and your God".' (Jn 20:17 NIV).

In her commentary Teresa spells it out. We are not only the

sisters and brothers of Jesus but of *each other.* This is the foundational commission that sums up the work of salvation. Church history begins here in the garden with the Risen Christ and Mary Magdalene. Because Mary proclaimed the news faithfully John was later able to insist, 'The commandment that Christ has given us is this: whoever loves God must love his brother also' (1 Jn 4:21 GNB). For John, as for his contemporaries, the word 'brothers' referred to those of his own race and kin. Now the ethnic barriers were down and his Letter included all Gentiles. As sisters and brothers there is no racism, classism, sexism; sharing goes across the nations and around the world. Any structures that aim to divide people, that tolerate relationships of domination/ subordination are sinful, contrary to Christ's work of salvation and the role entrusted to the Church.[3]

It is a world-wide experience that Christians have no difficulty in accepting God as father or sometimes as mother; the problem lies in accepting each other as sisters and brothers. Africans are community-minded; for them Mary Magdalene's message has meaning and African Christians believe that they have within their cultures, despite the upheavals on their continent, the sense of community that can restore to Christianity the Jesus vision of how people made in the image of God should live and relate. To continue in distorted relationships is to mock Christ. Third-world theologians insist that a new definition of Christian is needed. They no longer find it sufficient to say that the believing Christian is one who is baptised and professes Jesus as Lord. They suggest instead that a disciple of Jesus is one who tries to live the Good or God News of salvation by treating others as brothers and sisters.[4]

African women theologians insist that the creation of female and male has consequences far beyond biology, that Jesus though male did not ask us to image his maleness but his service, to 'wash each others' feet', to 'feed my lambs'. To focus on the maleness of Jesus and not on his service is to miss the whole point of his mission. They point out that in fact women understood that discipleship meant service and sharing long before the men (Lk. 8:1–3). After the rich young man turned away Peter asked, 'As we have left all, what will we get in return?' (Mt. 19:27). James and John not only objected to the healing powers of a man 'who is not one of us', but asked for the highest seats in the kingdom (Mk 9:38, 10:37). Even at the Last Supper they argued over who would be the greatest (Lk. 22:24). In Gethsemane Peter, armed with a sword, cut off the ear of Malchus, servant of the High Priest (Jn 18:10). On the road to Emmaus the two disciples who had fled told the unrecognised Christ that they had hoped he would have set up a new Kingdom (Lk. 24:21). Finally at the Ascension they asked: 'Lord, will you at this time restore the Kingdom to Israel?' (Acts 1:6 RSV).[5]

Third-world scholars find themselves frustrated by an interpretation of the Bible that is the product of a white, male, often celibate experience. Asian women theologians want to 'free the Bible and its interpretations from its age-old captivity by patriarchy, colonialism, and Western cultural imperialism'. They say, 'bourgeois European male theologians have standardised *common* human experience'.[6] Asian women's theology is born out of women's sufferings, not out of 'the logical consequences of academic debate' nor 'the pastoral conclusions of the institutional church'.[7] In Korea it is called *Han.* 'Han is a sense of unresolved resentment against injustice suffered . . . a feeling of total abandonment ("Why hast Thou forsaken Me?").'[8]

Suffering is also a theological source for women in Latin America. It is '. . . a Theology of Memory, counting crosses and resurrections . . .'[9] This 'subversive memory' is the key for, 'A future where women and men could walk together in community, and solidarity would flourish against individualism, lack of hope and indifferences.'[10] It is sometimes called a theology of blossoming.

Acting as Church for the World

When women's concerns were first raised in the Church they appeared under a title such as The Church and Women. Women objected to this as the title suggested that the Church and women were two separate groups. Then the title Women in the Church appeared, but this left some people imagining passive docile women. Women as Church has come to express how many Christian women see themselves as disciples of Jesus. The Church exists to carry on Christ's healing mission in the world and so committed Christian women are actively promoting God's reign of justice and peace.

Africa

Sisters in the Struggle to Eliminate Racism and Sexism (SISTERS) seek the support of the Churches in their struggle for justice. They claim that the increased breakdown in African marriages is not caused by women rejecting their maternal role but by their refusal to be subject to a husband. They condemn attitudes that suggest the life-giving biology of women is unclean and hold that to refuse Christian ministry to women on the basis of a Jewish ritual taboo is to deny the liberation Jesus brought to women. 'Do human beings have any further need to exist beyond the biological one of reproduction? Restricting women's lives to women's biology goes against the reason for being fully human, which is to reflect the fully divine as Jesus did.'[11]

For Jesus evangelisation meant wholeness. The poor to whom Jesus ministered were not necessarily economically deprived but were humanly so. Womanists see the Christian vocation as a challenge to the individual to become fully human. Therefore, the womanist movement is characterised by a concern for social justice. Those promoting the role of women in the Church are likely also to be involved with justice issues concerning world hunger, the just distribution of resources, the national debt, environmental abuse, violence against women and children, the arms industry and war, illiteracy, and so on.

Jesus said that he had come to bring life, life in abundance. Certain aspects of African culture promote this Jesus vision, for example: the extended family system with its sense of responsibility for the welfare of its members; the frequent family, village and group meetings at which each person is heard, compromise is expected and accepted, and consensus reached; the ability to live in harmony with nature; but most of all the African peoples' capacity to turn every ritual and occasion into a joyous celebration. Using these skills African women are dialoguing across religions, ethnic groups and social ranks in order to work together for justice. Throughout most of the continent they are succeeding in getting women's concerns on to the public agenda. A prior concern is the break-up of families and the vast increase in refugee camps.

The black women of South Africa were aware that they not only suffered with their men under racism, but also had to endure sexism as the men refused to the women the rights they sought for themselves. The women came together across the political divides and taught the men that they could not liberate themselves from the evils of discrimination and prejudice as long as they failed to extend to women complete equality in law and practice. Today in the new South Africa 24 per cent of those elected to parliament are women. This is one of the highest rates overall.[12] Issues on the women's agenda include a water tap in every yard, women's ownership of land so as to grow and sell produce, crèche facilities, clinics, and the abolition of the lobola. The lobola is the payment made by a bridegroom to the parents of the bride. In some situations (e.g. domestic violence) the parents refuse to allow the daughter to return home, as they do not wish to repay the lobola. In Kenya the Catholic Justice and Peace Commission has taken up the cause of women, of street children and of the tens of thousands of internal refugees.

Asia and the Pacific

Similarly in Asia the women's movement is influencing the Church's apostolic involvement. In Hong Kong the Catholic Justice and Peace commission has undertaken to study women's concerns and is networking with groups around the world collecting data and raising awareness locally. In the Pacific Islands where the dumping of nuclear waste is suspected of causing deformity in children, mothers are looking to the Churches to become involved in justice and peace initiatives. Coming from a culture that encourages subservience to the group, in which 'the nail that sticks up is hammered down', Japanese women are struggling to gain a sense of their own identity, psychologically and spiritually. The women call their movement JIRITSU which comes from the two words meaning 'self' and 'stand'.

Latin America

Across the Pacific the women of El Salvador expressed the same desire as their Japanese sisters when they called their archdiocesan women's programme: Women Learning to Stand on Their Own. In Latin America it is now realised that liberation theology did not take into consideration the position of women as women. When the sixth Feminist Latin American Conference was held in El Salvador in 1993 it sought to give autonomy to the women's movement which had supported the men during the war years. The political parties then in control were not addressing women's concerns. The El Salvadorian women who had fought in the war formed a new association called Women for Dignity and Life (The DIGNAs). They collaborate with women returned from the refugee camps in setting up small businesses for women, organise communal banking programmes, and get involved with building child care and community centres. In Grenada the legacy of slavery meant that black people were unable to establish a tradition of marriage. As a result few men take responsibility for their offspring, and women remain the sole providers for their children. The Grenada National Organisation of Women founded in 1994 strives to develop awareness, self-esteem and determination among women so as to enable them to improve their lot. The Latin American women look to white feminists to join them in their efforts to gain basic life-enhancing measures, such as piped water, literacy and land for housing

In Brazil women participate in labour unions, neighbourhood movements, mothers' groups and pastoral leadership. There a woman said, 'God is the force that won't allow me to surrender to the will of those who oppress my people.'[13] In Mexico women are interpreting what love means in a strict theological and social sense. They say among other things that

> Love means:
> – to participate actively in the building of new structures;
> – to collaborate for a better quality of life for all;
> – to sustain a persistent battle against an order contrary to the practice of Jesus and the Kingdom of God. [14]

In Argentina as women experience the tensions of the struggle they say, 'We have the opportunity to be not only participants in, but even agents of, this transformation that must take place if we are to be faithful to our very reason for being as Church.'[15]

Muslim Women

Originally, Islam was a liberating religion for women. With the introduction of the Koran into both the East and the West, local cultural interpretations were given to the text and often these proved very oppressive where women were concerned. The Sisters of Islam, a Malaysian-based women's group, have found the teachings of the Koran liberating, especially those dealing with the love and mercy that should exist between women and men. They are aware that extremists have presented a negative image of Muslims worldwide. Some believe that in order to keep the arms trade in place, sources in the West are trying to fabricate a new world enemy in the form of Islam. It is up to non-Muslim women to question anti-Islamic propaganda programmes.

A few years ago I attended an international women's conference in Dublin at which a young American journalist condemned the voluminous black chador and the yashmak she had seen worn by the Muslim women of North Africa, saying that men should have no control over what women wear. A Muslim woman present advised the journalist that she had perhaps misread the signs for, the explained, many educated Muslim women wear the chador to indicate their rejection of Western culture. Another speaker pointed out that many Western women slavishly follow fashions set by male designers, some of which are regarded as on a par with pornography. Apparently the wearing of the veil is sometimes an indication that women are taking their place in the public sphere and that they refuse to be confined to the home where the veil is not worn. Feminism is at times felt as a new form of colonialism, with Western women interfering in other cultures. Muslim women know how to negotiate within their own culture and find that Western women sometimes presume to know what is best for them.

The Moral Code

In discussions with young men and women I frequently meet a yearning for a stable moral code to prevail in society. Yet not one of these young men and women looks to the Churches to provide this moral leadership. Instead there seems to be a growing awareness that Church leaders, in assuming a monopoly over the whole area of moral guidance, have stunted the growth of a personally directed morality innate in each one: 'I will put my laws in their minds, and write them on their hearts' (Heb. 8:10 NIV). I was particularly interested to learn, from Chinese friends pursuing postgraduate studies in Dublin, that when organised religion was suppressed under the communist regime in China, many believed that personal morality would collapse. This has not happened, and parents, teachers, lecturers, managers and others in positions of authority constantly extol family and neighbourly co-operation, respect for the person and property of others, sexual restraint, honesty, hard work, etc.

Teresa Okure SHCJ believes it is the role of women to bring new hope to the world. 'The statement of John Paul II in *Mulieris Dignitatem* that women are in a very special way entrusted by God with new life has consequences for the Church as a whole, which may not be readily obvious, given the current tendency to identify the Church and the imaging of Christ with governance, power, control and guardianship of the deposit of the faith and the protection or safeguarding of apostolic traditions.' She goes on to explain that it was no mistake that when faced with death Adam 'named his wife Eve, because she would become the mother of all the living' (Gen. 3:20 NIV). Woman's God-given life-nurturing role, she says, takes on a new significance when humanity is confronted by calamity.[16]

Colonial oppression is now replaced by the oppression of the International Monetary Fund. If women thought globally and acted locally they could bring about a more just distribution of resources. The North/South, First world/Third world divisions have given way to two worlds, the world of the economically included and the world of the economically excluded. These two worlds have no geographical divisions: they are found within every nation around the globe.

Keeping in mind that Jesus came to give us life to the full, and aware that we are sisters and brothers to each other, it is important that women act together as Church and inform world leaders of their concerns. For it is only those who become aware who can bring about change. In the next chapter we will look at some of the issues of concern to women today. Womanists look to feminists to network with them across cultures so as to develop a common trust in each other, then together they can work for world justice and peace. Christian womanists firmly believe it is possible for women worldwide to move from Babel to Pentecost.

PAUSE FOR REFLECTION

1. Recall incidents when latent attitudes of racism, classism or sexism surfaced in your thoughts and words.
   (a) What triggered off these negative attitudes?
   (b) Can you in truth stand over them today? Why? Why not?
2. Whether you are a Christian or not, what does being a Christian mean to you?
3. Is your moral behaviour motivated by your inner conscience or by external rules?

9

BREAKING THE SILENCE

In every part of the world women are seen to be disadvantaged when compared with their male peers. Women are concerned about a variety of issues and women in different areas have different priorities. In Asia it is trafficking in women. In Africa it is agriculture and the provision of food. In Latin America it is literacy. In the post-industrialised countries it is political and economic equality.

Perhaps for women worldwide the move from Babel to Pentecost took place in Beijing in September 1995. It was there that the United Nations held its Fourth World Conference on Women, at which representatives from 181 states took part. Fifty kilometres away, in Huairou, around thirty thousand people attended the NGO (non-Governmental Organisations) Forum. It is estimated that the Conference and the Forum brought together over fifty thousand people to consider the concerns of women. The Beijing Conference was not so much a conference about women, as a women's conference about the state of the world in the closing years of the twentieth century. The Platform for Action, the negotiating document of the conference, was about gender, i.e. about the social and political relationship that exists between women and men. It did not regard women as a category apart, for the women's issues are in fact human issues, and our human oneness is now very much a planetary oneness. 'Looking at the World through Women's Eyes' was the overall theme of the 300 workshops and other activities organised at the NGO Forum, where participants shared and heard harrowing accounts of rape, sex slavery, trafficking and domestic violence.

As Peter Adamson writes in a recent UNICEF publication, 'there is a great silence around the suffering endured by many women because of their biology'. He describes how as a child a woman may endure genital mutilation, then when menstruating be treated as unclean. She may be married without her consent and become pregnant before her body is fully grown. If unable to bear children she may be abandoned or if she gives birth to a girl she may be abused. The work of his research team shows that each day around 50,000 young women and girls, using sharp sticks or knitting needles, attempt to abort themselves. Those who survive are left with pelvic diseases or crippling discomfort while the 75,000 who die each year do so in pain and alone, bleeding and frightened and ashamed. He concludes that, 'The silence around the suffering of many women needs to be broken.'[1]

The Girl Child

Many commentators when referring to humans divide them into men, women and children. This triple division ignores the great disadvantages suffered by the girl child. From the moment she is conceived the girl child can be discriminated against. So long as parents equate sons with survival and regard girls as a financial burden then the girl child is at risk. 'There are human communities in which discrimination against women begins even before they are born. Female children are not desired and violence may be done to the unborn girl, so she does not get born at all. In some communities the girl child does not even get fed or educated on the same level and equality as the boy child.'[2] During the social revolution in China male-female equality was a fixed tenet but when the one-child family policy was introduced in 1979 the abortion of female foetuses became widespread, so much so that in 1995 the Chinese government brought in legislation banning pre-sex selection. Today China has a surplus of abandoned girl children in state orphanages.

In the Beijing Platform for Action it was stated that the girl child was at a higher risk of dying before the age of five years than was the boy child, and that the girl child was less likely to be brought to hospital for immunisation and treatment than was her brother. It was estimated that the loss of girl children because of son preference is sixty to a hundred million worldwide. It was also held that the work burden of the girl child was much heavier than that of the boys in many countries around the world.[3] In some countries the girl child is denied an education, because her parents believe it is not worth their while to educate a girl. It was reported that today an estimated 130 million girl children have had no opportunity to attend school and that those who do attend are often withdrawn after a year or two in order to help care for their younger siblings.

> One of the great tragedies of third world poverty is the exploitation and abuse of children through child labour. Boys and girls, often as young as five and six, are put to work as carpet weavers or as gemstone cleaners . . . in clothing factories or in tanneries . . . making fireworks or baking bricks. Children frequently work a twelve-hour day for a pittance in poorly-lit, badly ventilated sheds, suffering eye strain and respiratory problems, and are exposed to hazardous chemicals. These children are often the sole breadwinner in a family, frequently 'bonded' to an employer to repay a parent's loan. Without schooling, they are trapped in a cycle of poverty, sacrificing their childhood, their health and their future. It is estimated that up to 200 million children worldwide are used as if they were slaves.

It is also safe to estimate that the vast majority of these slaves are girls.

Sex Abuse

There is a growing awareness of the hidden nature and extent of child sexual abuse in the West. Only about 10 per cent of incidents reported to the authorities are carried out by strangers; most are trusted adults known to the child. The children, especially the girls, are inclined to carry the blame, to be filled with feelings of guilt, as the abuse is seldom accompanied by threats but rather by bribes and the excitement of a secret shared with an older person. Abused children bed-wet, have nightmares, are disturbed, lose self-confidence, and very occasionally show precocious sexual behaviour. Children do not have the vocabulary to explain what is being done to them and when they try to tell they are often scolded and accused of looking for notice.

Submissive wives give no protection to their daughters who in turn become fearful and docile. This enables the father to become more and more authoritarian in all areas of family life. As she grows older and realises something is dreadfully wrong, the girl child is often put under pressure to remain quiet for fear the father is imprisoned and the family not only disgraced but impoverished. In Western societies girls who run away from home frequently cite incest as the cause.

The World Congress Against the Commercial Sexual Exploitation of Children held in Stockholm in August 1996 brought together for the first time policymakers and those working on behalf of children. One hundred and eleven countries were represented. The preparatory documents show the global extent of the exploitation, and the fact that children are often treated as commodities. Estimates indicate that more than 650,000 children, mostly girls, are involved in prostitution in Asia alone.

To avoid the HIV infection virgins are sought. This leaves young girls very vulnerable. Even their families give them into brothels in order to pay off parents' debts. Though sex tourism is big business, local men remain the biggest abusers of Third-world children. The extent of the Belgian paedophile network has shown that the protection of children has to be international. Australia, Belgium, Denmark, Finland, France, Germany, Iceland, New Zealand, Norway, Sweden, Switzerland and the USA already have in place legislation which enables governments to convict within the home country those who abuse children abroad. A report on the Stockholm conference warned that, 'We must get rid of the idea that it is just a few paedophiles, very different types of people, who are using child prostitutes. They come from a cross section of society; they are everyone.' Sad stories were told of girls who, having escaped from prostitution, were ostracised by their families and ended up living alone.

Another aspect of child abuse which needs special research is the involvement of religious people. In the 1980s and 1990s priests and religious brothers in Canada, USA, UK, Ireland and Australia have been taken to court as predatory paedophiles. Their victims were the children of friends, choir members, pupils and, the most vulnerable of all, those in their care. In September 1996 it was reported that police investigating alleged cases of child sex abuse against some Catholic priests and religious in Ireland began to suspect that they were dealing with a paedophile ring as witnesses told of how they were passed from one care-home to another. The state authorities were only too willing to hand over to religious the care of these children and seemed reluctant to investigate complaints. New research shows that paedophilia can be controlled but not cured. Therefore in some countries efforts are being made to ensure that in future known abusers will be isolated from all contact with children.

Genital Mutilation

While girl children in some areas of the world are used by male relatives for sexual gratification, in other places families obsessed with controlling their daughters' sexual nature subject them to horrific suffering. This is a very sensitive issue as the custom, which goes back more than two thousand years, is taken for granted in several cultures but is regarded as monstrous by the rest of humankind.

Female Genital Mutilation (FMG) is the name given to traditional practices which consist of cutting out part of the female genitalia. It may be restricted to a clitoridectomy in which the clitoris alone is cut out and perhaps the minor labia. About 15 per cent of girls subjected to this operation also undergo what is called infibulation whereby the greater labia is scraped and incised. The vulva, the entrance to the vagina, is then sewn so as to leave only a small opening. Of course, the purpose of the whole operation is to control the woman's sexual desires and behaviour. The daughter is presented to her husband as a guaranteed virgin who will not stray. For her sex will become a duty not a pleasure. Parents see themselves as acting responsibly when they put their girl child through this cruel torture.

The operation is carried out by older women called excisionists. If the practice is ended, their esteemed and paid position in society will be lost. It is therefore important to provide these women with training for other more acceptable medical services. While the excision and suturing is taking place the little girls, often as young as four but always before puberty, are given no anaesthetic and their legs are tied together until the wounds heal. Apart from the initial pain and shock the mutilation leaves the girl open to constant cramps and infection as it is difficult to pass urine and later menstrual blood. If there is uncontrolled haemorrhaging or if septicaemia sets in the result is death. Sometimes the urinary tract is damaged leaving the young woman with a permanent leak and bad odour, as happened to one bright teenager I taught in Nigeria. As young women, such girls are unable to get husbands, as are girls who have not been circumcised or incised. Where an infibulation has been performed, childbirth is difficult and the mother has to be cut open. Gynaecologists in England have described their horror when confronted with the small opening through which the baby is expected to emerge. Having cut the mother open in order to let the infant out the doctors were then asked to re-sew the vulva for the added sexual pleasure of the husband.

The World Health Organisation estimates that there are 90 million women alive today who have undergone these operations. An estimated 2 million girls are subjected to this mutilation each year.[7] Female genital excision is customary in parts of West and East Africa, the Middle East and Asia. In recent decades emigrant families have brought the practice with them into Europe and North America.

Probably the most dehumanising aspect of patriarchy is when women are credited with so little responsibility that their procreative powers are totally controlled by others. I have spoken with Western women who say they feel equally controlled and experience an overwhelming anger when women's bodies are made the objects of legislation by male legislators who fail to give equal attention to the male's responsibility in 'sowing his wild oats'.

Female genital mutilation is now recognised by the UN as a human rights issue, as an act of violence against a female. It is also regarded as a health issue. The campaign against female circumcision was started by Western feminists but is now prominent in women's concerns throughout the five continents. In 1990 Kenya banned all female genital mutilation. Since 1990 Burkina Faso has run a successful media campaign against the practice.[8] Canada has placed the practice on its criminal code. In 1985 Britain declared it illegal and girl children believed to be at risk are put on a protection register. However, some families get around these restrictions by sending their young daughters back to the home country to visit 'Granny'. In African societies where female genital mutilation is culturally based health workers avoid making any value judgments and instead focus their attention on the health of the girl child. They visit rural areas promoting good health practices. They believe government laws need to be supported by open discussion. Social attitudes are slowly changing and some men are beginning to refuse as wives women whose genitals have been mutilated.

No religion endorses the practice of female genital mutilation: it is a cultural practice. Some mistakenly say it is an Islamic requirement, which it most certainly is not. In the Somalia town of Luug a nurse arriving from Kenya saw at the hospital a constant stream of girls suffering from complications related to female genital mutilation. A devout Muslim herself, she went to the Imams at the mosque and pointed out that the Koran does not require female circumcision. It was acknowledged as a cultural, not a religious practice. Members of the Islamic Women's Organisation in the area were supportive. Talks were given and an education programme begun. Victims of the practice are found among Coptic, Protestant, Catholic, Moslem and Animist groups, yet no major religion has consistently spoken out against this cruel physical and psychological abuse of millions of girl children. Instead male religions still imply that women are created for the service of men and must be subject to them in both body and mind.

The transition into adulthood is very different for girls and boys, especially in its social implications. In some countries girls at their first menstruation are given in arranged marriages to men three times their age. These girls enter marriage without being consulted. They are often uneducated and undernourished. In Pakistan during a ten-month period in 1991, 2,000 young women died in dowry burning. These were put to death by the husbands or their families if the agreed dowry was not paid in full. Around 585,000 women die annually in pregnancy/childbirth disorders. It is estimated that 25 per cent of the women who die are teenage mothers. Maternal death is called the 'neglected epidemic' and in most cases could be prevented.

TRAFFICKING IN WOMEN

Trafficking in women is now a global industry crossing national borders and cultures. It is the result of poverty on the one hand and on the other of an affluence which allows men to enjoy a variety of sexual choices. It is sometimes referred to as the 'skin trade' or 'flesh trade' and is based on the sexual exploitation of women. Women in the poorer countries are targeted for organised prostitution and pornography. As these countries depend on foreign currency the Governments are tempted to turn a blind eye to the trade. European dealers import these women to meet the male customer demand. Sometimes the women are smuggled in without passports or work permits, or if they enter legally have their passports taken from them. In either case they are totally at the mercy of their masters.

In Holland a number of religious sisters, mostly returned missionaries, have formed an organisation called The Workgroup of Religious Against Traffic in Women. The sisters work to raise awareness among their own sisters and religious throughout the world, especially in those countries from which the young women are smuggled. To those latter they send leaflets for distribution warning families to investigate thoroughly any offers of well-paid jobs in the West for cultural dancers, artistes or even for domestic servants. At home they write articles and seek media interviews. Women who contact the sisters seeking help are given safe shelter and legal aid. Once a support club [illegible] to [illegible] the group informs [illegible] living nearby. The sisters [illegible] some [illegible] to give support to the [illegible] young women during her court ordeal. The group aims to establish a network of support both abroad and in the home country to enable the women to return to their families with some financial security and dignity. Through ecumenical groups the sisters challenge the Churches to speak out about this abuse of women.

There are in the world of prostitution and pornography those women who manage their own businesses. Their defiance can offer no excuse to a man when faced with a vulnerable young woman who has been trapped into the sex trade. Those ministering to women in the sex trade believe there is an urgent need for a [illegible] campaign to investigate how [illegible] and the women involved, and to question the attitudes of men who consider women's bodies a commercial commodity created for their consumption. Both prostitution and pornography objectify and dehumanise women. Men who [illegible] read about sexual activity in the pornographic magazines tell how they learned to equate sex [illegible] with the domination and control of women. It is [illegible] that women forced into prostitution in order to feed their children must be seen as part of the global exploitation of women [illegible] prostitution, tourism and pornography [illegible] society.

REFUGEES

Refugees form another vulnerable section of society. Forced from their homes and without passports they find themselves in alien lands unable to understand the local language. Of the 18 million refugees in the world today 80 per cent are women and children. 'Women suffer homelessness, displacement, they march up and down the continent of Africa and scramble onto boats in the hope of a safe haven. They suffer and die or are captured and dehumanised as refugees, victims of instability they did not cause. They suffer the results of inept governments run by men.' Speaking on video to the women gathered at the NGO Forum in Beijing/Hairou, Aung San Suu Kyi, the Burmese Nobel Prize Winner said that there has been no known instance in history when women have started a war. As refugees the women are not only exposed to poor nutrition and illness but also to sexual abuse.

Throughout history women have been subjected to especially brutal forms of rape during times of war. Rape as part of armed conflict has been documented in Bangladesh, Cambodia, Cyprus, Haiti, Liberia, Somalia, Uganda, Bosnia, Peru and Rwanda. An EU fact-finding mission into the former Yugoslavia estimated that over twenty thousand Muslim girl children and women were kept in sex camps and systematically raped, sometimes by soldiers acting under the orders and supervision of their military superiors. Thus the rape was made an instrument of war.[17]

The rape of women is at times used by men to humiliate other men. The woman or girl becomes simply a means to an end, a disposable object, and after their ordeal many commit suicide. This sexual violation of women destroys communities to such a degree that families find it hard to receive the victims back after the fighting has ceased. The courage of the Bosnian women in speaking out about their experience of war rape has enabled other women to come forward and tell of their sufferings. This is not an easy thing to do, and many women are not yet ready to face the fact that it was their fathers, brothers, husbands and sons who carried out such atrocities. The UN Security Council has recently, for the first time, declared war rape a crime against humanity.

Rape

Rape is a male disorder. Women are the victims. Even in peace time inadequate men seek out the bodies of women on which to vent their frustrations. Apart from the pain and trauma of the actual rape, many of the victims suffer socially after the event. In parts of South Asia raped women, if married, are accused of adultery. Many husbands have problems relating again to a wife who has been raped; there remains a niggling suspicion that she provoked it. Other women also criticise the unfortunate victim: 'Why was she wearing such a short skirt?' 'Why was she out so late?' But rape has nothing to do with women's fashions or the lateness of the hour. In Dublin, infant girls in nappies and elderly women in their homes or on their way to morning Mass have been raped. Rape is rooted in the desire to exercise control over another.

In 1991 the then Irish Council for the Status of Women organised a country-wide questionnaire to discover what were the main concerns of women. They were shocked to discover that for 92 per cent of the women surveyed the major concern was for their personal safety. They were afraid to go out alone at night or to be alone in their homes. 'Not for us the long walks in the parks, on the beach; or an hour spent in solitude beside a river.'

Many men on reading the above quote can truly say, 'I feel the same.' In fact police reports show that the most attacked person on the streets of Dublin is the young male, and usually at the hands of his own age group. For the reality is that over 94 per cent of violent crime is committed by men between the ages of seventeen and thirty-seven years. Why? It can hardly be accepted as normal human behaviour. It also means that males who are aggressively out of control are a costly burden on every national exchequer.

Most feminists accept that many men never abuse others, never allow their aggressive instincts to reach unmanageable levels, and that among them are men who support the feminist vision. It is the cultural attitude which accepts the aggressive male, idealises the macho image, that feminists *men and women alike* resist.

The relatively small number of women found guilty of violent crime have been released in some countries on grounds of abnormal pre-menstrual stress. This new attitude towards female violence has prompted men to ask if male aggression needs to be reconsidered. Research is now been carried out on the violent male testosterone and the term 'testosterone poisoning' is sometimes used.[18] Testosterone is associated with aggression as well as with the sexual drive. The female oestrogen has a neutralising effect on the male hormone and is regarded as a possible means of controlling the abnormal aggression activated in some men. Not everyone agrees with this line of thinking. Some women insist that rapists are not sick, that theirs is an acquired behaviour. They maintain that such men have been conditioned by a patriarchal and sexist society.

Institutionalised Violence

Feminists point out that a patriarchal society is a violent society where in practice 'might is right'. Violence means denying the equal common humanity of the other whether that other is an individual, a class, or a nation. It instils fear. Patriarchy has institutionalised violence and at times incited and used the aggression of young men. This century alone has seen over 400 million young men sent out to kill and be killed. They were expendable. Studies show that in 1988 there were over 200,000 boy soldiers fighting in twenty-five different countries.[19] Men too know what it is to suffer horribly as refugees or prisoners of war.

We have to ask why in the twentieth century do the poor of one country kill the poor of another country on the orders of their educated and wealthy leaders? While in prison in Northern Ireland Gusty Spence and David Ervine, both Unionist para-militaries, began to ask the same question. Among their fellow prisoners were young IRA members who shared the same financial and family concerns. Why were they killing each other? Who was pulling the strings? Both men are now active in a new political party working to break through old mind-sets and to bring mutual acceptance within their divided community. Violence does not solve problems. Eventually its instigators have to sit down at the negotiating tables.

Peace groups and feminists seek to establish a culture of negotiation, of conflict resolution through peaceful means. They lobby for the abolition of landmines which continue to maim and kill children and adults even after the treaties are signed. They ask for a curb on the arms trade and a reduction in military expenditure. Fifty years ago the United Nations organisation was set up to guarantee world peace, yet since then more than a hundred local wars have taken place. The big five (USA, China, Russia, UK and France) who are the permanent members of the UN Security Council and are entrusted with the supervision of the peace, are themselves the suppliers of as much as 86 per cent of the world's arms in an average year.[illegible] In Somalia US soldiers faced US weapons. In Rwanda large quantities of arms were supplied by the French. In Liverpool in 1996 a jury acquitted three women peace campaigners who, with hammers, caused over £1 million worth of damage to Hawk air-fighting craft about to be sold to Indonesia. They pointed[illegible] out that the public is calling for a ban on privately owned guns, yet the British government was selling death-dealing machines that would indiscriminately kill thousands of innocent people.[illegible]

DOMESTIC VIOLENCE

An important aspect of the Fourth World Conference on Women is that for the first time the UN treated domestic violence against women as a crime, as a human rights issue and no longer as a private family affair. Any local custom, tradition or religion that condones a husband 'disciplining' his wife' is to be opposed. It is often forgotten that the most dangerous place for many women and children is not in the street but in the home.

In the UK, violence in the home 'accounts for nearly a quarter of all reported violence and affects one in four marriages regardless of class, creed or culture'.[illegible] Children who witness parental violence suffer long-term emotional harm. In the USA domestic violence is the leading cause of injury among women and poses a greater threat than cancer to their lives.[7] At Beijing it was reported that 58 per cent of Japanese women suffered physical abuse from a partner.[8] These beatings can consist of head banging against a wall, attempted strangulation, kicking when on the ground resulting in internal injuries and abortions. Roddy Doyle has written a prize-winning novel about a battered wife; it is called *The Woman who Walked into Doors*. In Dublin, instead of wearing dark glasses, battered women explain their bruising by saying 'I walked into a door.' It is estimated that only about 2 per cent of domestic attacks are ever reported and that each woman endures an average of thirty-five beatings before seeking help. The police and social workers warn that once violence begins in the home and is accepted it becomes more frequent and violent. Meanwhile the abuser may appear in public to be a devoted family man. Men of every class, race and religion [illegible] women in their place.

A woman does not have to be beaten to be battered. For some the act of intercourse is used to humiliate and degrade. Some suffer sexual and emotional abuse so that self-esteem is destroyed. They are shouted at, criticised, belittled in front of others and called stupid, ugly and fat, and are expected to clean up after their husbands at all times. People removed from the problem show a complete lack of understanding when they ask, 'Why doesn't she leave him?' Others blame the woman for the violence, [illegible] [illegible] [illegible] courage and independence on the part of the woman [illegible]. Most battered women have to make [illegible] for their [illegible] with [illegible]. It would seem that lack of [illegible] is not a [illegible] factor in the case of [illegible] violence. The [illegible] business woman [illegible] at home because of her [illegible] and [illegible] character.

[illegible] recognise the extent to which their lives have been controlled by fear. They then enable them to build up self-esteem and learn to regard their husbands as equals; only then can change take place. Many of these women had been [illegible] as an end in itself, their ultimate achievement, and had endured their sufferings in order to maintain their status.

Towards the end of the 1980s some men in Ireland recognised that they had a problem and formed a support group called 'Men Overcoming Violent Emotions' (MOVE). They operate a telephone helpline, hold regular seminars and meetings, and are supported by psychiatrists. They learn that violence is not the only response, that they have options and responsibilities. Groups are now active among men throughout the country. People concerned for the children of violent men hold that the parents' separation should not lower the children's standard of living; that the children should continue to live in the same house and attend the same school. This thinking has led women to question the position of battered women who fled their homes with their children. It has been suggested that the refuges for battered women should be turned into hostels and treatment centres for the abusers. The men could continue to go to work and receive family visits. In this way home life for the children would continue in a more normal routine, free of the threat of violence.

Financial Dependency

The majority of families living in poverty worldwide are headed by a woman who is widowed, divorced, separated, deserted, unmarried, or who has fled from a violent situation. In fact it has been pointed out that most women are only one man away from poverty – which led to the remark: 'There seems to be a presumption that God gave women wombs and men wallets.'

The stereotype of the woman cared for and financially supported by a loving hard-working husband has not only burdened men, but has put many women at a grave disadvantage both at home and in the work place. When in 1891 Pope Leo XIII wrote his social encyclical *Rerum Novarum*, he argued in favour of a 'family wage' for men. Women were seen as dependants. In that same year in the USA there were several million women in the workforce, many of whom were in the professions and some under fifteen years of age.[25] Yet their situation was not acknowledged. In Ireland wife dependency was actually legalised. The allowance for couples on welfare was paid to the husband.

When a man does not regard his salary as a 'family wage' he can resent having to support another adult and may distrust her spending of his money. Financial dependency leaves wives very vulnerable. Feminists aim at achieving economic independence for all women, but are divided on how best this can be achieved. Some seek equality of training opportunities and pay. Many women would like to attend women gynaecologists, psychiatrists and lawyers, thus indicating that there is a need for more women in these professions. Some say that the lack of child care facilities is in fact the greatest glass ceiling encountered by women in the work place. Other women prefer to put their energies into getting economic and legal rights for women employed in the home as carers of children. However, women in the home often care not only for children but also for dependent adults. Generally this unpaid work of women as carers in the home does not feature in the national GNP. In some countries it is estimated that home-carers contribute up to 39 per cent of the GNP.

A growing number of men and women believe that a basic income for all would provide the simplest solution. It would do away with the complicated systems of welfare, grants and allowances and would drastically change the financial dependency relationship between women, men and adolescents. For the past decade several European groups have been studying various proposals for the financing of such a scheme. Financial dependence for food, housing and clothing forces many a woman to play the role of the helpless wife, and this subservience feeds into the man's authoritarian approach and even into his battering behaviour. When a battered wife finally flees from her violent situation she comes face to face with the reality of her own poverty. Then in order to secure her children's education she returns to the home and becomes more passive than ever. When questioned, one much-battered wife explained: 'There are two reasons why I stay. One is eight and the other ten years of age.'

THE RELIGIOUS DIMENSION IN DOMESTIC VIOLENCE

Though theologians have struggled with the issue of violence in relation to war they have been reluctant to name domestic violence for the evil it is. Instead it is an issue that is often trivialised.[26] Christian marriage should be a prophetic symbol in the world, a sign of Divine Love, but many women know that not all marriages between Christians are sacred signs; for them marriage has been an endurance test, a facade, and they wonder if it ever had a sacramental moment. For many Catholic women the Church is seen as part of their problem. They believe that Bible texts have been used to legitimise the domination/subordination relationship within marriage. In Genesis 3:16 Eve is told that she is to be subject to her husband as a punishment for her sins. The Gospels never preach such a message. In the Letters attributed to

Paul we read, 'Wives submit to your husbands in all things, as you would to the Lord' (Eph. 5:22). 'Wives give way to your husbands as followers of Christ, this is your duty' (Col. 3:18). Husbands have used such texts to justify their violent behaviour and women have remained in physically dangerous situations because of their religious beliefs. A man who commits violence against a woman can say, 'the Bible confirms my belief that men are the head of the household'. Women recovering from violence may say, 'It is God's will'.

Over and over again priests have told women that to refuse a husband is a sin – this to wives who were battered and bruised. As recently as 1998 I heard a priest, preaching at Mass, exhort wives who were beaten to unite their sufferings with those of Christ on the cross; he offered them no safe shelter, no [illegible]. Women in Africa accuse Church men of ignoring their plight. 'When women suffer rape and sexual harassment, church men pass by on the other side.' The silence of women in the Church is only surpassed by the silence of the Churches with regard to violence against women.

In his Apostolic Letter on *The Dignity of Women* John Paul II declared that the passages already quoted from Ephesians and Colossians describe the stratification of relationships that prevailed between men and women since the fall, [illegible] and that Christ redeemed this sinful situation and restored to women and men their original equality. In 1994 the Vatican at the request of the Irish hierarchy gave permission for alternative readings to be used on the days assigned to the passages concerned. A statement from the Catholic Press Office said that the Irish bishops sought the permission because the particular passages [illegible] may be [illegible] understanding and [illegible] today.

FOR YOUR REFLECTION

1. Do you think the [illegible] violence [illegible] by some men is [illegible] and should be [illegible]? Why?
2. How would you assess women's responsibility for the present state of male/female relationships?

10

Woman, Symbol of Life and Hope

[illegible]

and development programmes. At a meeting in Scotland, East European and Hawaiian women were guests of a Christian women's group, exchanging advice on social issues. The women of the Dublin Rape Crisis Centre successfully lobbied their government and were sponsored to give five training programmes in rape counselling to community workers in the former Yugoslavia.[3] The Working Women's Forum in India has mobilised 280,000 women in programmes for self-improvement. Around the world there is a marked increase in the number of women benefiting from first-, second- and third-level education. In China alone 70 per cent of women now read and write and their enrolment in third-level education has increased tenfold.[4] Trade unions have become more active in support of women's rights, and in the area of health, research has begun into ailments specific to women. Over the past twenty-five years much has been achieved by the women's movement.

The Beijing Platform for Action is like no other UN document. For the first time the girl child is mentioned in her own right. Women are no longer treated as a separate 'problem', and the rights of women are firmly placed within the category of human rights. Violence against women is at last on the public agenda. The document calls on all signatories to promote women's economic independence and freedom from poverty by providing equal access to resources including land, credit, technology, training, employment and markets, and rather than start a separate fund to meet women's needs, countries were asked to reduce their military budgets and channel the surplus money into supporting the development of women.

Great international declarations are useless unless implemented by each national government. So during the next few years it is up to all those concerned with justice, especially in the Churches, to put pressure on legislators to pass the necessary laws. With goodwill such legislation could be in place by the end of the millennium. A hopeful sign is that women's concerns will never again be off government agendas. The theory that women could be 'fitted in' to a patriarchal agenda was flawed. A new approach has begun. Feminists are accused of having empowered women to speak out on many fundamental issues without having first educated them to understand how divergent possible solutions might be. The Platform for Action recognises that progress has been uneven. This means that women have to continue working to build bridges between classes and races as well as between the sexes.

Already more and more men are becoming aware of the extent to which the patriarchal structures have legitimised injustices towards women. Men interviewed on a *vox pop* section of a TV show said the women's movement was the best force for change this century. Another wished women were given equal rights without having to struggle for them. Yet another believed feminism was a necessary phase in self-discovery for both men and women.[5]

RELIGION AT BEIJING

'Men have hijacked our religion and turned it against us.' This sentiment was expressed in a workshop attended by Hindu, Buddhist, Christian and Muslim women at the NGO Forum near Beijing. They pointed out that culture and tradition had shaped religions through the centuries and that it was necessary for women to study the sacred books for themselves. A Muslim woman was applauded when she suggested that women of all religions should study together in order to develop a spirituality which would be more life-giving for women.[6]

The tension between universal rights and cultural or religious rights came to the fore with the question of equal inheritance for the girl child. The Muslim representatives interpreted Islamic law differently. The proposal was put forward that 'Girls and boys have the right to an equal inheritance.' This was seen by some as contrary to the Koran and was reworded as; 'Girls and boys have an equal right to inheritance.' Among some Islamic peoples the sons' portions are greater as they are expected to care for their elders.

The Vatican delegation to the Conference was led by a USA law professor Mary Ann Glendon and included women from the other continents. Many of the international delegates felt that the Vatican misunderstood and mistrusted women, interpreting their demand for control over their own bodies as selfish and depraved. Professor Glendon said that the Vatican supported responsible parenthood and that women should oppose any practice which encouraged men to be sexually irresponsible.

A great many feminists do not support abortion and remind women that it is usually the female foetus that is targeted. Abortion is seen as a sign of failure. They hold that women have the responsibility to develop a successful sex education programme, to plan, and to practise self-discipline. At Beijing it was accepted that abortion should not be promoted as a method for family planning.

Women as Church

In her book *Woman Strength*, Joan Chittister OSB uses the event on Tabor to illustrate two approaches to Church. Jesus had taken Peter, James and John up to the mountain to pray. There Jesus spoke to neither priest nor king, but to two prophets: Moses who had led his people out of bondage, and Elijah 'the trouble maker of Israel'. On seeing Jesus transfigured, Peter wanted to stay and build booths (read: institutions). But Jesus led the disciples back down the mountain to where a [illegible] in the form of an epileptic [illegible] needed healing.7

The prophet has the dual role of criticising and energising and the signs are that this is the role women are called to in the Church today. Just as Church leaders reacted to the Reformation by centralising power in Rome, [illegible] and [illegible] climate of [illegible] today a similar reaction is taking place to the [illegible] of [illegible] that [illegible] from the Second Vatican Council [illegible] people to take some responsibility for their own salvation.8

It is [illegible] women within the Church who [illegible] the [illegible] vision of a faith community. These women are [illegible] in bringing Christ's healing to others. They enable [illegible] and women to [illegible] with their own spirituality, help them to become informed [illegible] familiar with the Gospels and confident in [illegible] that has gone unquestioned for centuries.

[illegible] his life on earth Jesus did not [illegible] priesthood [illegible] the [illegible] the [illegible] prophetic [illegible] in the early Church [illegible] the [illegible] of the Church [illegible] Jesus Christ [illegible] vision of a more [illegible] and just society.

At [illegible] the [illegible] women [illegible] many [illegible] mentioned in this book, such as the [illegible] preservation of the environment, the just distribution of land for food production, the [illegible] of [illegible], [illegible] of [illegible] for women to [illegible] and [illegible], the spread of the AIDS [illegible] the promotion of literacy [illegible] and the distribution of [illegible] to keep [illegible] with [illegible] world. As one Ugandan woman explained, 'I [illegible] about [illegible] because my parents [illegible] me that it is only men who [illegible], just like eating chicken and eggs.' Bishop [illegible] of Nakuru, Kenya has described how when he saw the needs of his people for water, health care, technical training and so on. He was convinced that this type of human development was an integral part of the Good News of Jesus Christ.[illegible]

As Church we need to support all agencies working for a more just world and to lobby governments for the implementation of agreements reached at Beijing. The Platform for Action recognised women as a basis for leadership in [illegible]. Peace at local and global level was seen as linked with their empowerment and their inclusion in decision-making.

The insights of Christian feminists are leading Church officials to an awareness that there is a whole untapped source of spiritual life which [illegible] in the realisation of Christ's prayer 'that they may all be one' (Jn [illegible]). Whatever their race or class, many Christian women are now [illegible] on their rights as on their responsibilities to Church and society. With newly-won confidence, they are undertaking study and research and learning communications and lobbying skills so that they can work effectively for change on earth [illegible]

[illegible]

sharing and justice are coming to the fore.[10] We cannot change the past but the future is ours to shape.

There is no future in apportioning blame: together laity and clergy are caught in the present system. In mutual trust we can create a climate that will enable shared responsibility, as we come to accept that we are a Church of the baptised. Then each one will be recognised as participating in the mission of Christ, and the leadership of the bishop will be seen as the centre of unity in the diocese or local Church. Ordination does not bestow management, financial and sound decision-making skills, but all the skills necessary reside within the community as a whole.

While some are fearful, others experience a new upsurge of hope as they join in the study, prayer and research now taking place in universities, conferences and house groups all over the world. For Christian feminism and womanism is not only about justice for women, but about reclaiming the Gospel, the Good News for all. Speaking at the Synod of Bishops 1983, Archbishop Vachon of Canada described it as an advancement in civilisation, a step forward in bringing the reign of God on earth.[11]

Women in the Church need to help each other to overcome their traditional passivity and undertake the responsibility of working, together with their brothers, to secure justice with compassion for all irrespective of race, class or sex. The Beijing UN Conference on Women is ended; the work of ensuring that its Platform for Action is implemented locally has just begun.

Final Word from Pope John Paul II

Addressing the members of the Vatican delegation on the eve of the Beijing Conference the Pope said:

> I appeal to men in the Church to undergo where necessary, a change of heart and to implement, as a demand of their faith, a positive vision of women. I ask them to become more and more aware of the disadvantages to which women, and especially girls, have been exposed and to see where the attitude of men, their lack of sensitivity or lack of responsibility may be at the root.[12]

Pause for Reflection

1. List groups you believe Jesus would associate himself with today, in order to further God's reign on earth.

Are you surprised at any of the inclusions or omissions on your list? Why?

2. 'The most loving thing a slave can do for his master is rebel.' Why?
   How would this saying apply to a committed Christian within:
   (a) the Church,
   (b) society?

NOTES

3. Teresa Okure SHCJ, Talk given to the Holy Child community, Dublin, 17 November, 1994.
4. Ibid.
5. Teresa Okure SHCJ, *The Role of Women in the African Church*, SEDOS 25, June/July 1993, p. 169.
6. Chung Hyun Kyung, *Struggle to be Sun*, SCM Press, 1991, pp. 107–108.
7. Ibid, p. 22.
8. Ibid, p. 42.
9. Marcella Althaus-Reid, 'Doing the Theology of Memory: Counting Crosses and Resurrections', *Life Out of Death*, Best and Hussey (eds.), London: CIIR, 1996, p. 196.
10. Ibid, p. 206.
11. Mercy Oduyoye, 'Violence Against Women: A Challenge to Christian Theology', *Journal of Inculturation Theology*, Vol. 1, No. 1, Port Harcourt, Nigeria: CIWA, 1994, p. 49.
12. Pauline Eccles, 'Women and Development', *75/25 – Ireland in an Increasingly Unequal World*, Dublin: Dóchas, 1996, p. 95.
13. Ivone Gebara, 'Women Doing Theology in Latin America', *With Passion and Compassion*, Fabella and Oduyoye (eds.), Orbis Books, 1994, pp. 163–4.
14. Maria Pilar Aquinas, 'Women's Participation in the Church – A Catholic Perspective, *With Passion and Compassion*, Fabella and Oduyoye (eds.), Orbis Books, 1994, pp. 163–4.
15. Nelly Ritchie, ibid., – A Protestant Perspective – pp 157–8.
16. Teresa Okure SHCJ, SEDOS 25, art. cit.

CHAPTER 9

1. Peter Adamson, 'A Failure of Imagination', *Progress of the Nations 1996*, UNICEF, p. 4.
2. Mercy Oduyoye, 'A Challenge to Christian Theology' from *Journal of Inculturation Theology*, Vol. 1, No. 1, 1994, Port Harcourt, Nigeria: CIWA, 1994, pp. 38–9.
3. Pauline Eccles, 'Women and Development', *75/25 – Ireland in an Increasingly Unequal World*, Dublin: Dóchas, 1996, p. 98.
4. *Facts and Figures*, UNICEF, 1996.
5. Tracy McGeogh, 'The Scourge of Child Sex', pp. 1126–27, *The Tablet*, 3 August 1996, pp. 1126–27.
6. See Susan Mckay, 'Irish Clergy in Child Sex abuse Ring', *The Sunday Tribune*, 22 September 1996, pp. 1 and 10.
7. Pauline Eccles, art. cit.
8. Christopher Brazier, 'The Razor's End', *New Internationalist*, June 1995, pp. 13–15.
9. *Annual Report 1996*, UNICEF, p. 63.
10. Liam Wegimont, 'Religion and Development', from *75/25 – Ireland in an Increasingly Unequal World*, Dublin: Dóchas, 1996, p. 251.
11. *Facts and Figures*, UNICEF, 1996.

12. *What is Christian Marriage*, seminar sponsored by Sophia/Dublin, 13 February 1993.
13. *Addressing Sexism: A Franciscan Challenge*, Lesson Unit 24, p. 15.
14. *Facts and Figures*, UNICEF, 1996.
15. Mercy Oduyoye, 'A Challenge to Christian Theology', from *Journal of Inculturation Theology*, Vol. 1, No. 1, 1994, Port Harcourt, Nigeria: CIWA, 1994, p. 43.
16. See Helen MacLaughlin RSJC, 'Two Key Words: Tolerance and Sustainability', WUCWO (World Union of Catholic Women's Organisations) Newsletter, December 1995.
17. Angel Robson, 'Rape: Weapon of War', *New Internationalist*, June 1993, pp. 13–14.
18. See 'Don't Hang it on Hormones', *The Irish Times*, 4 February 1994, p. 11.
19. *Facts and Figures*, UNICEF, 1996.
20. Caitriona Ruane, *Bringing it all Back Home*, Bejing Report from Fermanagh Women's Network, 1996, p. 15.
21. See *The Tablet*, London, 3 August 1996, p. 1032.
22. See *Catholic Woman*, National Board of Catholic Women, UK, Pentecost 1995, pp. 4–5.
23. Nikki Van der Gaag, *The Word*, Ireland: SVD, Roscommon, August 1996, pp. 4–6.
24. Steven Mufson, 'Women of the World make Common Cause', *Washington Post*, 24 September 1995.
25. Claire Murphy SHCJ, 'Patriarchy', from *Modern Women*, December 1992, Meath Chronicle, Ireland. p. 4.
26. Mercy Oduyoye, see Note 2, Chapter 9.
27. See Michael O'Sullivan SJ, 'Christianity and Violence against Women', Irish Commission for Justice and Peace, Report of Study Day, October 1995.
28. Mercy Oduyoye, *Journal of Inculturation Theology*, Port Harcourt, Nigeria: CIWA, April 1994, pp. 45–6.

CHAPTER 10

1. Tereas Okure SHCJ, *The Role of Women in the African Church*, SEDOS 25, June/July 1993, p. 167.
2. Caitriona Ruane, *Bringing it all Back Home*, Bejing Report from Fermanagh Women's Network, 1996, p. 15.
3. See *Healing the Trauma of Rape and Sexual Abuse*, Dublin Rape Crisis centre report, 1994.
4. Caitriona Ruane, *Bringing it all Back Home*, Bejing Report from Fermanagh Women's Network, 1996, p. 11.
5. 'Comely Maidens', 16 February 1995, RTE 1.
6. Magda Frijns, 'Religion and Culture = Force for Women?', WUCWO (World Union of Catholic Women's Organisations) Newsletter, December 1995.

7. Joan Chittister OSB, *Woman Strength*, Sheed and Ward, 1990, pp. 74–6.
8. See Gillian Gaudbug FSVM, *Catholic Woman*, Newsletter of the National Board of Catholic Women UK, Pentecost 1995, p. 6.
9. See 'Roman Bishop praises Irish generosity', *Trocaire World*, Spring 1996, p. 3.
10. Donald O'Mahony MSC, at a course given to SHCJ sisters in Mayfield, Sussex, August 1989.
11. Archbishop James Hayes, Address, Synod of Bishops 1988. See Canadian Conference of Catholic Bishops, *Study Aid on Women in the Church*, 1995.
12. Pope John Paul II, *L'Osservatore Romano*, 30 August 1995.